HAUNTED CITY

Tom Slemen

The Tom Slemen Press

Copyright © 2015 Tom Slemen

All rights reserved.

ISBN-10: 1516869524
ISBN-13: **978- 1516869527**

For
Dr R. I. King
Vir bonus et ridiculam medicum

CONTENTS

Introduction	1
The Sefton Park Vampires	10
That's Me Over There	26
Second Skin	30
Hilty	43
The Little Old Lady	56
The Geometry of Death	74
The Wind from Hell	78
The Night Mare	86
Back from the War	93
Long-Distance Beatle Ghosts	96
Black Spider	101
A Lovely Old Lamp	106

The Damned	112
The Devils in the Wine Cellar	121
Little Devils	130
Crossed Line	135
The Red Menace	145
The Ouija	157
Phantom Road	171
A Warning from Beyond	176
Buyer Beware	192
Ghostly Replays	198
Shining Eyes	211

INTRODUCTION

Liverpool - so much has been written about this wonderful place but, in my opinion, not enough of its supernatural history. Some years ago I put forward a suggestion of great potential to Liverpool City Council. At the time there were plans to turn the former Irish Centre - which had been lying derelict for a decade on Mount Pleasant - into yet another hotel; in this case, a hotel with a modern plate-glass frontage. Surely this Grade II listed building should be preserved, I argued, and not have its unique and imposing frontage destroyed, as planned? No reply from the dullards. The council rhetoricians love spouting about culture, whilst neglecting Liverpool's own culture. My idea was simple yet important; that we should have a repository of Liverpool folklore housed in the Irish Centre, which would have its interior renovated for this archival purpose. Researching material for my books over the years I have collected many oral traditions and amassed pages on forgotten characters from Liverpool (as well as Lancashire, Wirral and Cheshire) folklore. I have also unearthed many a tale that local historians have overlooked - such as the unsolved murder of Elizabeth Peers in 1905. the ghostly vestiges of the

David Eccles murder of 1891, the Madge Kirby abduction and murder, and even eyewitness accounts of the leaping terror - Spring-Heeled Jack, to cite but a few.

Running parallel to the conventional history of Liverpool - from King John granting the town a charter in 1207, to the history of the docks and the regeneration of the city centre — there is an unseen seam of supernatural stories that have been largely ignored by the strait-laced historians, with their lacklustre approach to the teaching of history.

Take, for example, the history of witchcraft in Liverpool. As far as I know, I am the only author who has written about the Castle Street covens of the seventeenth century and the expulsion of their witches to the outskirts of the town. If you have always harboured the feeling you don't fit in, or are different from everyone else, you may have witch (and warlock) DNA in your genetic make-up. You may even be a descendant of that enigmatic supreme witch Jenna Green, whose statue, unearthed at St James's Mount in the late Victorian period, has long gone missing, given away by an Irish navvy to a Woolton man to adorn his garden. Some think Jenna is responsible for the legends of that childhood bogeywoman, Ginny Greenteeth.

A good few years ago an old man visited me during a two-day local history weekend at St George's Hall, put on by a local radio station. The man asked me if I had heard of a strange incident in which a boy fell down a quarry in West Derby and survived but became transformed into a prophet of some sort by his injuries. I replied that I had indeed heard the story and would fill in the details once I had consulted my notes, kept at home in a box-file. An eavesdropping know-all local historian on the neighbouring table sneered at the old man's recollections, but I wiped the smile off his face on the following day, when I produced an old booklet entitled *Stories and Customs of Old West Derby*, written and published by Canon HE Crewdson, Rural Dean of West Derby. On page 26 of this booklet, Canon Crewdson detailed the story which the elderly man had enquired about and he returned on the Sunday to St George's Hall to read all about it. Here's what he learned: The church of St James, in West Derby, was quarried from the 'delf. The word delf, derived from the Anglo-Saxon word 'delfan' which means to delve or dig, was situated between Quarry Road and Uppingham Road, and in the year 1902, when this strange incident took place, the delf was 250 feet deep. One day in that year, an unusually large and robust Rhode Island Red rooster was perched on the edge of the delf, looking down at the quarry pit, when five-year-old Georgie, who was said to have learning difficulties, rushed forward and grabbed the bird's two legs. The rooster spread its huge wings and, squawking and screeching, it flew forward a little in its vain bid to escape the clutches of the miniscule mischief-maker.

Both bird and boy fell the 250 feet but, through some miracle of providence, what should have been a fatal fall for the child, was broken somewhat by the frantic flapping of the rooster's mighty wings, and Georgie landed without a scratch at the bottom of the quarry. The bird was also uninjured but fluttered away from the infant dare devil and hid in a crevice.

The boy was spotted on the quarry floor by a passerby and the alarm was soon raised. A farmer was lowered down to the child on a rope and Georgie, and eventually the rooster, were rescued. However, the parents of the five-year-old quickly noticed a great change in his personality. Before his hair-raising descent, the only two words Georgie seemed to be capable of uttering, were 'mam' and 'dad', and he would emit the occasional grunt to express displeasure. But after the incident at the delf, he began to talk in a strange voice with an adult vocabulary and what's more, he began to make a number of prophecies, all of which came true.

The first predictions concerned a number of deaths that would occur locally and these deaths all came to pass, which greatly disturbed Georgie's parents and the local folk of West Derby. It is said that Georgie also predicted the outbreak of World War One and foretold the horrors of trench warfare, describing the millions of deaths in horrific detail. Alas, the boy's eventual fate is unknown, and he doesn't get a mention in the annals of Liverpool's conventional local history.

Another supernatural omission from the history of my hometown is that of the Tower Ghost. This amorphous apparition, which usually materialised in the north-east bastion of Liverpool Tower, was said to assume a variety of terrifying and appalling forms, and had on several occasions scared the tower's soldiers and was a sentinel to approaching death.

The entity is documented in several obscure tomes on the town and also in the *Liverpool Mercury* newspaper for August 1816. The demonic-looking ghost seemed hell-bent on terrifying people in the tower, which once stood at the shore end of Water

Street, and was the home to the Stanley family for many years. The Tower Buildings stand on the site of the old tower today. Unfortunately, the local historians are of no help in telling us what became of the Tower Ghost.

Another paranormal anomaly that you won't find in any Liverpool local history book is the mysterious 'Greenstone' of Sefton Park. Like some grim forgotten sentinel of yore, the stone stands to the southern end of the lake, where the paths fork. It was placed at that location in Victorian times, shortly after it was found embedded in the clay by workmen digging the foundations for a school in Edge Hill. It weighed eight tons, was five feet in height and six feet in length. "A giant must have carried this stone here," the foreman joked to the diggers, probably unaware that a vast sheet of ice had, in fact, brought the colossal stone down from Scotland many millions of years ago when the woolly rhinoceros, Giant Deer and Mammoth walked the hills of Liverpool.

Not long after the 'Greenstone' (as it was nicknamed, because of the thick layer of moss which covered it) was placed in Sefton Park, some people claimed it glowed with a faint aura as twilight gathered. Then, in July 1886, a blind girl named Rose Williams was taken to Sefton Park by her Aunt Elizabeth, who wanted the ten-year-old child to enjoy the fragrances of the flowers.

Late in the afternoon, Elizabeth decided it was time to take Rose home, especially since some out-of-season rainclouds had suddenly blotted out the sun. All at once there was a flash of light - and it seemed to emanate from the ancient boulder.

"What was that?" asked a startled Rose, turning towards the Greenstone. Although she was totally blind, the girl claimed she had somehow 'seen' the flash of light in her mind. This, despite the fact that in the past she had heard rumbles of thunder, but had never once 'seen' lightning flashes. Was her sight returning? A doctor sadly ruled out that possibility, but on the second occasion when Rose visited Sefton Park, she experienced what she described as a "kaleidoscope of beautiful colours" in her mind's eye, when in the vicinity of the Greenstone, whereas her aunt saw nothing.

Elizabeth didn't see the flash, yet a couple strolling up one of the paths on the south side of Sefton Park lake froze as they beheld a brief glare of blue light. A week later, Rose asked to be taken to the Greenstone again, and once more she 'saw' light coming from the prehistoric boulder. Aunt Elizabeth again saw nothing, but the flash opened up a kaleidoscope of blazing geometric colours in the mind's eye unfortunately followed this time by terrifying images of strange monsters and serpents. Rose fainted when she beheld the frightening visions, and was never allowed to visit the Greenstone again until she was an adult, and it is not known if she 'saw' any further visions emanating from the stone.

However, the visions of the Greenstone are not confined to a Victorian blind girl, for I received letters from two people (unknown to one another) who wrote to me in response to a potted history of the Greenstone I once broadcast on Radio Merseyside. A Mr James Lawler of Knotty Ash wrote to me first, to tell of a very intriguing incident which took place in

1937.

James Lawler was about fourteen when he and a group of friends were playing in Sefton Park one late afternoon. One of the lads came running up to Lawler crying, "Jim! Look at this!" He led Jim and the other five lads over to a boulder, over the surface of which they saw faint shadowy shapes moving about. Jim then described what seemed to be a dinosaur. "Just like the one King Kong punched," was how he described it, referring to the Tyrannosaurus Rex in the famous 1933 landmark fantasy film. After a few moments all the mysterious images on the boulder faded away. Could the dinosaur seen by the children on the Greenstone be one of the 'monsters' the Victorian blind girl had perceived around the boulder in 1886?

In 1967, a man whom I shall call Mr Smith, also witnessed an extraordinary mirage at the Greenstone. He had just left Madame Andre's Turkish Baths on Ullet Road, and had decided to go for an invigorating stroll through Sefton Park. Another witness joined him on that pleasant evening, a young woman whom I shall refer to as Miss Jones - a nurse from the nearby Sefton General Hospital Nurses' Home. Mr Smith and Miss Jones were walking hand in hand along the path near the lake, when they witnessed an undulating green glow above the Greenstone. "It was like a miniature show of the Northern Lights," Mr Smith told me, and described greenish-yellow streams of light (possibly ionised air) drifting up from the boulder.

That same year, Miss Jones recalls, scores of children reported seeing glowing green fairies in the park, and she believes the ethereal little people had something to do with that glowing rock. We may discover more about the Greenstone some day, but if the orthodox historians had their way, the Greenstone mystery would almost certainly be omitted from the chronicles of Liverpool as historians tend to present a version of history which leaves little room for inexplicable oddities and shocking legends.

A case in point is that of King John, who, as I stated earlier, announced the foundation of Liverpool in his charter of 1207, and was even said to have designed the layout of Liverpool's first seven streets.

One wild stormy October night, in the year 1216, King John died - most probably from dysentery, but many still maintain he was poisoned - and he was entombed at Worcester Cathedral. And now for the part the history books never mention. Shortly after King John had been laid to rest in his grand tomb, terrible howls and snarling sounds were heard echoing through the vastness of the cathedral, and these unearthly noises were plainly coming from King John's tomb. Pious monks were called upon to deal with the appalling sounds, and they evacuated the church and exhumed the former ruler's body.

The corpse presented a terrifying spectacle, for it had changed out of all recognition, and its now misshapen mouth now sported large canine incisors and pointed wolf-like ears. The monks quickly declared that King John had been a werewolf, and had the Plantagenet monarch's remains removed from consecrated ground and buried in a nearby common at a crossroads, where suicides were buried face down with stakes through their midsections. The body of a pauper was put inside the king's tomb, and was draped in a damask robe with a sword placed in its hand. The tomb was then resealed, but the rumour of the royal werewolf got out somehow and has never been quashed to this day.

It would be ironic indeed, if it turned out that Liverpool had been granted its 1207 charter by a werewolf!

> Tom Slemen,
> Liverpool,
> England

THE SEFTON PARK
VAMPIRES

I have collected too many reports, interviewed too many people, and seen too many strange things to confidently doubt the existence of vampires. Common sense seems to rule out the idea of Dracula-like beings, although common sense is notoriously unreliable. In 1895, the supreme mathematical physicist and engineer Lord Kelvin, the President of the Royal Society, stated that common sense told him that any machine heavier than air could not fly under its own power, but within a decade, the Wright Brothers were taking off in their early powered planes. In 1970, Margaret Thatcher's common sense led her to state that, "No woman, in my time, will ever be Prime Minister of Great Britain," yet, of course, just nine years later, in 1979, Mrs Thatcher became Britain's first female Prime Minister.

What the inexperienced amongst us would perceive as vampires are, perhaps, unclassified parasitic beings of many species. Some seem to be substantially corporeal and solid, whilst others appear to be gaseous and invisible. They come and go as they please, the physical carnate ones siphoning the blood from their victims, while the phantom-like discarnate types drain the life-energy of their prey. The victims are usually left haemoglobin-deficient and often inexplicably lethargic, even though they have had more than enough sleep. Doctors, in their ignorance, will diagnose the victims' maladies as anaemia, or Chronic Fatigue Syndrome, also known as ME (myalgic encephalomyelitis).

Over ten years ago I was very surprised when a priest I had known for many years told me that he had once tackled a vampire that was troubling his parishioners in a certain district of Liverpool in the 1980s. "It looked half man and half beast," the priest told me, "and when I confronted it in the bedroom of an elderly couple, it vanished before my eyes. I held out a crucifix to the thing and bid it never to return. Over the course of a fortnight, the vampiric entity would puncture the leg of the old woman as she lay in bed and stealthily suck out her blood. The woman and her husband were often struck with a strange temporary paralysis when the being - which they only perceived as a shadow - commenced its bloodsucking."

An older priest in another parish suggested that I should hang bulbs of garlic in the window of the old couple's room as a deterrent. I followed his advice and the thing never returned. I was afterwards urged by a senior figure in the Archdiocese not to mention the vampire incident to anyone, as it might be damaging to the Church. I later heard that a similar creature - possibly the same one - was making nocturnal visits to a house on Granby Street.

What follows is a strange tale about mysterious beings that could have been vampires, told to me by a retired doctor a few years ago.

At 7.30pm on the Monday evening of 30 October 1967, two medical students, Duncan and Richard, left the lounge of the YMCA on Mount Pleasant, after watching the latest episode of the popular police drama series, *Z Cars*. Duncan and Richard, who were both aged twenty-four, were lodging at the YMCA, and on this chilly autumn evening they left the building and embarked on a journey to their friend Murray's flat on Brompton Avenue, just a stone's throw away from Sefton Park. The three men had recently started seeing three young women who lived at a large shared flat at a house on Ashfield Road, Aigburth Vale, and they set off together to visit them.

Murray, who was also a medical student, had the bright idea of taking a short cut through Sefton Park. The three students strolled through the parkland at 8.35pm, and noticed that a ground mist was forming all around them, which lent an eerie Cimmerian mood to the shadowy autumnal acres. Within five minutes, the ground mist had crept up to their waists, and was as thick and cold as concentrated dry-ice vapour. Murray was complaining of having a cold and was just asking Duncan if he could borrow his scarf, when a woman's scream from somewhere in the distance startled them.

"It came from over there, I think," said, Murray nodding towards the bowling greens in the murky distance, but Richard had an acute sense of hearing and knew that Murray had mistaken the echo of the scream for the real thing. "No, it came from over there - come on!"

Richard led the way, trotting off through the swirling mist towards the ghostly-looking Palm House which was looming darkly through the haze, like some great stranded spaceship. Another scream - a little fainter this time - was heard by all three. It was definitely coming from the small forest of trees on the east side of the park, in the direction of Mossley Hill Drive. Murray pointed out some movement in the mist, and the three of them raced to the aid of the woman. What they came upon was extraordinary and quite unexpected.

A young blonde woman of about twenty or so was lying in the arms of a pale-faced middle-aged man, who wore an outlandish long dark cloak, and was biting into her neck. "Oh, my God!' gasped Murray, when he realised that the man was not kissing the young woman's neck, but sinking his fang-like teeth into it. The whole scene was like something out of a cheesy horror movie, but they could all see that the woman was in grave danger. She was no longer screaming and putting up a fight, and had become limp in the man's arms, as if she had fainted.

Startled by the sudden intrusion, the vampiric fiend looked up with that sly guilty look of an animal devouring its prey, the bloody evidence of his crime smeared all over his chin. He stared at the three terrified students for a couple of seconds, then dashed the woman to the ground and ran off at an incredible speed, his cape flapping dramatically behind him. His ghostly figure was quickly consumed by the fog.

Duncan and Richard picked up the young woman and propped her up against a tree. The situation was even more critical than they had thought, for arterial blood was spurting out of her neck in regular bursts, and they called for Murray, who was still peering into the fog, as if he expected the weird attacker to return at any minute. Duncan told him to find a public phone box on the periphery of the park and call for an ambulance. Murray sped off and was lucky enough to find one fairly quickly. In those days, vandalised telephone call-boxes were a rare occurrence, and when Murray located a red call-booth, it even had an intact telephone directory on its shelf. He dialled 999, requesting the ambulance service, and gave vague directions to the scene of the peculiar, but life-threatening, attack, "That's right, Sefton Park - close to the Palm House - just to the east of it - come quickly. " Duncan pinched the woman's neck wound to try and stem the bleeding, and presently the victim - whose name was Sandra - regained consciousness but was very weak and incoherent. She remembered being snatched and then dragged into the park from Greenbank Lane after being half throttled. The ambulance duly arrived, and the three students accompanied Sandra to the Royal Infirmary, on Pembroke Place. A surgeon cleaned up Sandra's neck wound and then stitched it up. She was also given a tetanus jab and kept in hospital for observation for three days. The police later interviewed her, and then quizzed the three medical students, in an effort to get a useful description of the bizarrely dressed neck biter. As the attack had taken place on 30 October - the day before Halloween - the police arrived at the conclusion that the Sefton Park attacker had been dressed in a Halloween vampire costume. Perhaps it had just been a practical joke that had backfired, with the prankster getting carried away and biting Sandra's neck a little too hard.

Today, 'Mischief Night' - when children believe they are entitled to play dangerous pranks on adults - is observed by the ill-behaved on 31 October, but in 1967, no such celebration of warped humour existed.

Sandra had felt her lifeblood being sucked out of her neck by the man, whom she judged to be in his fifties. He had very dark penetrating eyes and the black slicked-back hair above his temples was streaked with grey. It was a terrifying ordeal.

The infamous 'Summer of Love' had preceded that autumn, when hippies and a considerable section of the everyday population of the world had turned to psychedelic drugs and polyamory, in a bid to break free of a society fettered by outdated laws and customs. Drug-taking was rife, especially the taking of LSD, which induced all sorts of weird and disturbing hallucinations, and it transpired that Sandra, the girl who had been bitten on her neck, had dated a man who had been arrested for taking LSD a few months previously. The police would have viewed this fact with considerable suspicion, and may have hypothesised that Sandra herself had either hallucinated the vampire, or even been attacked by her ex-boyfriend while he was on some psychedelic trip.

On October 31 there was a Halloween party at the house on Ashfield Road where the medical students' girlfriends shared a flat. A young couple, Harry and Elsa, held the party in the upstairs flat of this Aigburth residence, and Richard, Duncan and Murray arrived at the bash at around 8.15pm. In those days, Halloween was known as Duck-Apple Night, and it did not have the same occult overtones as it does today. However, as the night drew on, the wine flowed and the music eventually stopped at around 2am. A thick fog enveloped the house in a white icy vaporous void, penetrated now and then by the occasional moan of a distant foghorn on the river, or the disembodied voices of people down in the street.

Thirteen people lay or sat in a rough semi-circle around the glowing embers of the coal fire in the grate. Duncan and his girlfriend Judy sat snugly side by side in an old two-seater sofa, both mellow from the bottles of ruby Burgundy they had consumed. Murray sat alone, slouched on a multi-coloured patchwork beanbag in the corner, sipping a brandy as Jane, his girlfriend of six months, was in the toilet downstairs being sick from a gin binge. Richard was sitting on the windowsill smoking a Woodbine cigarette as he chatted to his girlfriend Mandy about his plans to buy a car. Richard's attention alternated between Mandy's Maya-blue eyes and the dense fog swirling beyond the window panes. He kept thinking he saw figures in the street down below, but they vanished as quickly as they appeared, making him think he had imagined them, which was not surprising, considering the quantity of spirits he had consumed earlier. Mandy watched him squinting and screwing up his face as he peered into the fog.

"What's the matter?" she asked. "You seem really edgy all of a sudden. Have you seen something down there?"

"Oh - nothing," replied Richard, distractedly, "only I thought I saw a group of people down in the street for a moment - must have imagined it - too much booze!"

Mandy cupped her small hand against the window pane and scanned the fog. She could make out nothing but the dim suffused lamplight, coming from the far end of the street, and the vague undulating outlines of the gateposts down below.

Murray's partner Jane then returned from the toilet

looking the worse for wear, with a wide-eyed shocked expression on her face.

"What's up, love?" Murray asked. "You look as if you've just seen a ghost!"

"I've just seen faces at the toilet window downstairs." Everyone in the room could see that Jane was having trouble keeping control of her emotions and keeping the quiver out of her voice.

"Faces? What kind of faces?"

Murray put down his brandy glass and got up to face his nervy-looking girlfriend. Jane grabbed his hand and held on to it for reassurance. "Whoever they were, they couldn't see much because they were looking through frosted glass, but their faces looked really pale - as if they had pan stick make-up on."

Murray rushed over to the window with Jane in tow. Down below were five mist-enshrouded outlines of people down below, standing on the pavement in front of the house. One of them was wearing a long cape, and to Murray he appeared identical to the uncanny attacker who had bitten Sandra on the neck the night before. Richard and Duncan wondered what Murray and Jane were staring at and they in turn came over to the window and looked down into the nebulous murk and also saw the five menacing outlines assembled in front of the house. Soon, Mandy, Judy and the seven other people in the room were crowding at the window to take a look at the five strangers in the fogbound street.

Harry and Elsa, the couple who had hosted the party in their upstairs flat, mentioned that there had been a number of attempted burglaries in the area in recent weeks. Maybe this lot were casing the joint. Harry opened the window, letting in the salty-tasting fog. "Hey! You lot down there! I've just called the police, so clear off!"

The figures did not react in any way. The four pale-faced men, who were all wearing dark suits, still stood facing the caped man, as if mesmerised by him. Murray, Richard and Duncan were now absolutely convinced that this man was the 'vampire' who had struck in Sefton Park the night before.

"Actually, I really am calling the police," Elsa told her husband Harry, and she hurried over to the black telephone on the table in the corner and dialled 999. There was no tone in the earpiece. The line was dead. This was a new and worrying development, because it suggested that they were being targeted in some way. The room fell quiet as each person looked around to the others for reassurance. The temporary calm was broken when Jane and Mandy each let out a scream as a man's hand shot through the open window and grabbed the edge of the inside sill. His head then loomed into view. The head belonged to a man in his fifties with bloodshot eyes - the very unsavoury character who had sunk his teeth into Sandra's neck in the park.

Judy instinctively slammed the window down heavily on the stranger's wrist and he let out an animal cry of pain. He then quickly withdrew his hand and tumbled back into the fog. Harry acted quickly, closing the window securely and fastening the catch. He then turned to Elsa, snatched the telephone from her hands and tried to call the police himself, but as Elsa had already told him, the line was completely dead. Harry, like everyone else, suspected that one of the weirdos outside had cut the phone line, but what for? What sort of sinister plan did they have in mind? There were no mobile phones in that day and age, so there was no way of alerting the police to the unearthly quintet laying siege to them outside - short of running all the way to Lark Lane Police Station.

Elsa drew the curtains and then hurried to the other room, which overlooked the back garden. She pulled the curtains together there too. How on earth had the man with the cloak managed to scale the wall to the window on the first floor within seconds? That was the crucial question that everyone at this after-party wanted answered. No one was in any hurry to leave with those five creepy strangers still lurking about outside, especially the ultra-agile one.

Those present sat hushed fearful whilst Murray gave an account of the 'vampire' attack in Sefton Park, which was corroborated by Richard and Duncan. Their alarming story, together with the fog and the lateness of the hour, combined to stir the macabre imaginations of both hosts and guests alike. Just then Judy emitted a yelp and jumped back into the room, after taking a peek through the drawn curtains. She told her friends that she had seen the head and shoulders of one of those people outside floating past the window. The face was grotesque, yet almost clown-like with the contrast between its livid whiteness and its dark-rimmed eyes.

A rather refined-looking guest who had been reclining on the sofa for most of the evening, communicating with virtually no one, suddenly stood up in front of the dying fire. His name was Gareth Ingam and he was studying architecture at university -

that much his friends knew - but for many years he had also studied the Occult, and vampires in particular. He calmly told the other guests and his hosts that the five 'people' outside were actually vampires, which caused quite a stir of mixed reactions. One guest named George, a muscular rugby player from Runcorn who was related to Elsa, gave a hollow laugh, "Oh, come on! There's no such thing as vampires," he said, scornfully, "so let me go out there and give those idiots a good hiding. Harry, have you got a cricket bat I can borrow?'

"I'm afraid I haven't, George," Harry replied, without taking his eyes off the vampire expert.

"You'll need more than a cricket bat to tackle those things out there," said Gareth sneering at George, and he then made a great show of undoing his shirt to reveal a silver crucifix on a chain. "They thrive because of our ignorance."

Murray and Duncan took a peep through the curtains and immediately Duncan smiled and visibly relaxed. He told them all what they all wanted to hear. "Well, folks, it looks like Count Dracula and his gang have finally gone home to their cemetery. Yep, they've definitely gone."

"Of course they haven't gone. They'll be lurking about in the fog," said Gareth, in a low sombre voice as he looked at his crucifix. "Seriously, my advice to you all is that you should stay put till sunrise."

"Oh, for Pete's sake, Gareth! Could you kindly shut up, mate?" said a highly annoyed Murray, who was trying to persuade his terrified girlfriend that it was all just a bit of a prank. "Vampires only exist in horror films. It's nineteen sixty-seven - not sixteen sixty-seven. Can't you see you're scaring the girls?"

Duncan tried to calm his friend down with a small shake of the head, "Okay, Murray, take it easy - Gareth was just joking, you know." But the expression on his own face showed that he too was ill at ease.

"I can't stand him at the best of times," Murray whispered into Jane's ear, as he pressed his face into her curls. "He's a real know-it-all. He thinks he's it."

The group was silenced again when the handle of the door suddenly squeaked loudly. Everyone froze. The door opened about ten inches, and a ghastly skull-like head with black cavernous eye-sockets peeped in at them. Jane screamed, wrenched herself from Murray's embrace, and crouched down in a corner, where she tried to conceal herself behind a chair. Everyone drew back from the horrifying visitor - all except Gareth Ingam, who bravely walked towards the ghoul, taking off his crucifix as he did so. He thrust it at the skeletal face and said something in a language which sounded like Latin. The monstrosity spat gobbets of vile-looking dark saliva at him, before beating a hasty retreat on to the landing outside. Judy started to scream, and Elsa held on to Harry as if she were about to pass out.

Gareth slammed the door shut and leaned against it with his back. Immediately, there came a heavy thump on the other side of that door which shook Gareth, and he shouted frantically to Murray to bring an armchair over to the door. A bookshelf full of weighty tomes was then hoisted across the room by Duncan and Richard, and placed on top of the armchair. Still the thing outside battered relentlessly on the door, but after a few minutes, the thuds suddenly stopped. In the long uneasy silence which followed, the thirteen people remained cooped up in the room all night.

At 5.30am, a waning hair-thin crescent moon rose in the east, followed, almost an hour later, by the sun. A milk float rattled its way down Ashfield Road not long afterwards, as thirteen weary people poured out of the house in a huddle, including Harry and Elsa, who took their valuables with them in two suitcases and went to stay at a friend's home in Widnes. Judy, Mandy and Jane also found new accommodation at a flat in Kensington.

Gareth Ingam told Duncan, Richard and Murray that he intended to track down the five vampiric beings, and he even asked if they would help him, but they flatly refused. The three of them had been thoroughly traumatised by the events of a Halloween they would never forget. A part of them still wondered if the whole incident had simply been some elaborate prank, but what about the man who bit Sandra's neck in Sefton Park? and the impossible 'levitation' of the same caped fiend up to the window of the house on Ashfield Road? Not to mention the fiend who had tried to gatecrash his way into their party.

Years later, in 1971, Duncan bumped into Gareth in Chester. By now, the amateur vampire hunter was a fully fledged architect. He told Duncan that he had lain in wait in Sefton Park on several nights, during November 1967, hoping to spot the vampires once again, but had witnessed nothing. Then, the day before Christmas Eve of that same year, as he was out shopping in Church Street, he had noticed a vaguely familiar figure amongst the crowds. It was the caped man who had seemed to levitate up to the window of the house in Ashfield Road. He was dressed quite normally on this occasion, in a sheepskin coat and tweed trousers, and he was walking out of Hepworths the tailors. He headed towards the crossing on Hanover Street, and Gareth followed him.

He trailed him up Bold Street and into Chinatown, where the man with grey streaks in his hair met an oriental gentleman outside a tobacconists called Foggos. They talked for a while, and then the Chinese man was seen to bow respectfully to him before he left. Gareth still shadowed the stranger as the late afternoon darkened, and every step of the way he expected the thing to turn around and look at him. He tried to keep a hundred yards distance between himself and the suspected vampire at all times and almost lost him on Windsor Street, but he spotted him again standing in the doorway of the Napier public house - and now he was staring straight at him!

Gareth panicked and darted into a newsagent for a few moments to regain his composure, then took a quick look out, and saw the man walking over to Admiral Street. Gareth hurried after him, and at last he saw the man enter a fine Victorian house on Belvidere Road, not too far from the convent there. He kept watch on that house for a few days over the holiday period. Having lodgings on nearby Aigburth Road, it was not too much trouble to keep the place under surveillance for an hour or so every now and then. He soon deduced that the man lived alone but had two regular visitors on Fridays. These were peculiar-looking individuals in their thirties, with skin as pale as his own and invariably dressed in black suits.

Gareth then hatched a hare-brained scheme. He wrote a letter which he addressed to 'The Vampire' and sent it to the house. In the letter, Gareth claimed he was about to go to the police to report perverted and life-threatening acts of vampirism — unless he was paid a hundred pounds. The man was to meet him on a Monday evening at 8pm at the White Lion pub on Great George Place, off St James Street, not far from the Anglican Cathedral. Gareth naively envisioned the 'vampire' immediately doing as he was bid and going to this pub, thus giving him an opportunity to break into the fiend's house, in order to gather evidence of his despicable deeds.

The ruse did not work, and instead, something quite unexpected happened as a result of him sending the blackmailing letter. Gareth crept into Belvidere Road one evening to find a bunch of children making a nuisance of themselves on the steps of the bloodsucker's home. The front door of the house was wide open, and a few of the children were shouting and running about in the hallway. All of a sudden, one of the children ran outside and fired a stone from a catapult at an upstairs window, spectacularly shattering it. The noise brought an old man out from the house next door and he shouted at the vandal and the boy ran off as his friends cheered.

A police car arrived minutes later, and upon its arrival, the children careering about in the house scattered in all directions in the gathering twilight. Only then did Gareth realise that the vampire's house was now no longer occupied. It seems that he had moved out in such a hurry, that he had left all his furniture, carpets and curtains behind.

On the following day, Gareth visited the old man who had chased the children from the abandoned house and asked happened to know where his former neighbour had moved to. The old man was a little reluctant to talk at first, and kept looking up and down the street to make sure he was not being watched. He claimed that he knew nothing about the man who had lived next door, nor any of his friends whom, he had noticed, had always visited him at night, mostly on Fridays. He then whispered about something the police had allegedly discovered in the cellar next door - bottles of congealed human blood. Gareth checked with the police to ascertain if this was true and they, in turn, eyed him with suspicion and asked him why he wanted to know. Was he a friend of the man who had lived at the house on Belvidere Road? Gareth told a policeman at the local station about the vampire attack in Sefton Park and the events on the night of the party, at which the constable shook his head in disbelief and told him to "Hop it!"

And there the peculiar case of the Sefton Park vampires ends — at least for now. I have already written about 'Manilu', the so-called 'Lodge Lane Vampire' in another of my Haunted Liverpool books, as well as stories of other vampiric beings. Are all these accounts merely the product of overactive imaginations, or are vampires really at large in this city and beyond? Perhaps a secret society of such beings exists right here under our very noses. If that is so, then the more we choose to disbelieve in them, the more vulnerable we become.

THAT'S ME OVER THERE

Early in October 1863, the *City of Limerick*, a Royal Mail steamship of 1,339 tons, sailed out of Liverpool bound for New York. Amongst the passengers on board were Mr SR Wilmot, a Connecticut manufacturer who had numerous business dealings in Liverpool, and his sister Eliza Wilmot. Sharing a stern berth with Mr Wilmot during the voyage home, was an Englishman, William J Tait, a librarian in his fifties.

Two days out from Liverpool, the fierce Atlantic winds whipped up a severe storm that was to rage, almost without a break, for nine long days. The usual delights of a trans-Atlantic voyage were all but abandoned, as one passenger after another succumbed to that scourge of the ocean cruise - seasickness. Wilmot soon fell victim to the misery of seasickness himself and lay groaning in his berth for days on end, enjoying very little sleep in the storm-tossed steamer. However, on the eighth night of the storm, the howling winds abated somewhat and the sea calmed for a while, and Mr Wilmot was able to enjoy a few snatches of well-deserved sleep.

At around 4.15am that morning, Wilmot sank into a deep slumber and had a strange dream, in which his beloved wife entered the cabin, dressed in her white nightgown. Mrs Wilmot came over to her husband and knelt at the side of his bunk and began kissing him on the lips. The dream was so realistic that he could actually feel his wife's lips pressing upon his. She smiled longingly at her husband and then quietly left the room.

When Mr Wilmot awoke, he was startled to see the librarian, Mr Tait, gazing quizzically down at him from the upper bunk across the cabin. Tait then made a peculiar remark. He said, "You're a pretty fellow to have a lady come and visit you in that way."

"I beg your pardon?" said Wilmot, deeply affronted and perplexed by Tait's words.

The librarian explained his comment by saying that he had been lying awake on his bunk, also trying to suppress his nausea, when he happened to notice a lady he had never seen before, come quietly into the room. She had been dressed in a white nightgown, and she had kissed Mr Wilmot as he slept, just as in his dream. The woman had certainly not been Eliza Wilmot, the businessman's sister, whom Tait had been introduced to previously, as they were boarding the ship. Mr Wilmot did not know how to respond to Tait's strange confirmation of his dream and was at a loss as to what to come up with by way of explanation.

On 22 October the *City of Limerick* reached New York, and after negotiating the gang-plank rather unsteadily, a relieved Mr Wilmot made his way to the home of his wife's parents at Watertown, Connecticut, for that was where Mrs Wilmot had been staying with her children as she waited for her husband to come back across the Atlantic. Not long after his reunion with his wife and children. Mr Wilmot began to tell them that he had experienced a very peculiar dream during his trans-Atlantic voyage, upon which Mrs Wilmot interrupted her husband with an intriguing question, "Did you receive a visit from me on the morning you had that dream?"

Mr Wilmot was flabbergasted. His wife told him that she had heard the news about a ferocious and prolonged Atlantic storm that was forcing a ship called the Africa to run aground off the shore of St John's, Newfoundland, and so she naturally worried about her husband's safety aboard the *City of Limerick*. Mrs Wilmot had been so consumed with worry that she had found it impossible to settle down to sleep as she lay in her bed on the eighth night of the storm. She wished with all her might to be with her dear husband, and at around four in the morning something very uncanny took place.

She seemed to float out of her bed and travel through the darkness outside towards the ocean. She flew across the raging storm-swept seas and after some time, when the wind had briefly dropped somewhat and the heavy clouds had parted, she saw, by starlight a long black ship, trailing a thick plume of steam, cutting its way through the heaving swell. Mrs Wilmot willed herself up the side of the three hundred and thirty-one-foot-long steamship and flew on to the deck.

She somehow found her way to the cabin and drifted along in a dream-like state until she reached the doorway of a room where a stranger was sitting up in his bunk, studying her with an expression of great interest. An oil lamp burned nearby and by its light Mrs Wilmot saw her husband sleeping on the other bunk, and she felt compelled to enter the cabin. She went to her husband's side, knelt down, and kissed him as he slept. To corroborate her story, Mrs Wilmot was then able to describe the cabin in every last detail to her shocked husband. After kissing him and reassuring herself that all was well, she had then drifted back across the sea to her home and her own bed, and the next morning she had told her mother all about the peculiar, though highly realistic 'dream'.

The case was later investigated by the Society for Psychical Research, and although Mrs Wilmot's journey was never properly explained, it is possible that she experienced an unusual type of what is known as an Out of the Body Experience (an OBE).

In times of illness, or great stress - and sometimes even when the person is perfectly fit and well - people have reported experiencing the sensation of travelling out of their body. It has been widely reported in people undergoing major surgery, for example, and individuals involved in car crashes and other serious accidents have also described their consciousness peeling off and floating away from their physical body. However, it is very rare for a person's non-physical body to be seen during an OBE, and yet Mrs Wilmot was seen by Mr Tait as she was visiting her husband. This leads us to another possibility; that Mrs Wilmot 'bilocated', a phenomenon which we shall explore in the next story.

SECOND SKIN

Bilocation, in which a person appears to be in two places at one time, is a phenomenon that has been reported many times over the years. In most instances of bilocation, the double appears solid, although it is rare for them to speak and even rarer for them to attack their flesh and blood counterpart, but this is precisely what happened in the following account, related to me by the woman mentioned in the story.

In the summer of 2006, thirty-five-year-old Jaclyn was living alone in a flat on Liverpool's Georgian Canning Street, and spent most of her days contemplating the disastrous way her life was going. Jaclyn had recently moved into the flat after being beaten-up a few weeks previously, though not for the first time, by her violent husband Chris and left with a black eye and a broken finger.

One Friday night during this period of personal turmoil, Jaclyn went to visit her friend Claire, who worked as a barmaid at a pub in the city centre. At the pub she met a very attractive and younger man of about twenty named Craig, and became so drunk, both with the alcohol itself and the youth's affection towards her, that she kissed him passionately in front of all the other customers. Claire was a bit worried about Jaclyn's wayward behaviour, because it was so out of character for her to flirt with someone who was fifteen years her junior. She was normally a rather quiet, proper and reserved person, but the drink had obviously lowered her inhibitions. When Claire followed Jaclyn into the pub's toilet to advise her alcoholically-liberated friend to "calm down" a little, Jaclyn accused her of being jealous, from which point things quickly escalated. "Claire, can I just tell you something?" Jaclyn asked, drunkenly pointing her finger in her friend's face. Her speech was slurred and very loud. "You think you're the bee's knees round here, don't you? 'Ooh! Look at me! I'm Claire - the glamorous barmaid!' but you're just that, just a little barmaid, Claire, and that's all."

Claire was quite unprepared for the bitchy remark and was deeply hurt. She had known Jaclyn since they were in junior school together and knew that she had always been a good friend to her and vice versa. In a broken voice, she replied, "Look, Jackie, no one is jealous of you, and I know I'm just a barmaid - I've never professed to be anything else - so where did all that come from?"

Jaclyn shook her head and put her hand to her mouth to stifle a loud burp, then pushed Claire aside and staggered into the toilet cubicle. Claire could hear her being sick into the toilet bowl, so she knocked on the door and asked if she was alright. Jaclyn swore back at her, then rambled on about Claire having more friends than her.

"You're drunk, babe," said Claire, her ear close to the cubicle door.

"A friend to everybody is a friend to nobody," was Jaclyn's reply.

When Claire returned to the bar, the other barmaid who was on duty that night, an older woman named Marie, said there had been "a bit of a fight" between Craig - Jaclyn's young admirer - and another man. They had both left the pub in the middle of a slanging match.

When Jaclyn came swaying back into the bar and saw that Craig was no longer there, she asked a few of the drinkers where he had gone. One of them mistakenly believed he had been thrown out of the pub for fighting, and so Jaclyn immediately jumped to the conclusion that Claire had sent him packing in a fit of jealousy. The air turned blue with Jaclyn's foul-mouthed outburst, and Marie the older barmaid, a rather well-built woman, grabbed Jaclyn by the collar and marched her to the door, where she was ejected unceremoniously into the street. Jaclyn stumbled along for a few hundred yards, crying and muttering to herself, then continued the remainder of the journey home barefoot, as her new high-heeled sandals were cutting into her toes.

The next morning she awoke with a pounding headache. She gulped down glass after glass of water to rehydrate her brain, and with a mounting sensation of dread she began to remember bits and pieces of the disastrous events of the night before. Had she really encouraged the attention of a twenty-year-old lad? And had she really said all those horrible things to Claire? It was definitely time to apologise, so she rooted through her handbag for her mobile phone, but was unable to find it and nor could she find her purse. She struggled to recall the journey home from the pub; was it possible that she could have dropped them out of her handbag without noticing? Even though she had been so drunk she didn't think she had, as the handbag had been securely fastened when she came to it that morning. She suddenly had a terrible gut feeling, and that sensation was rarely wrong - that Craig had stolen the purse and mobile at the pub.

Jaclyn turned her living room and bedroom upside down but the purse and phone were nowhere to be found.

She had only lived in the Canning Street flat for a few weeks, and, relying on a mobile phone to keep in touch with friends and family, she had not had the landline telephone connected yet, but she urgently needed to ring Claire to apologise and tell her about the possible theft of her mobile and purse, which had contained eighty-five pounds. She found some loose silver change in a drawer, and after putting on some make-up and getting dressed, she set off for the public telephone box on Catharine Street. She paused, recalled Claire's home telephone number, and dialled, inserting a twenty-pence piece. Claire was not available and her telephone answering service kicked in.

Jaclyn was in a quandary as to what to do next. Should she get a taxi to Claire's home in Huyton? Yet how could she? She had no money for the taxi fare, and her debit and credit cards were both in her purse, which had probably been stolen. She decided she would have to go to her bank on Lord Street and make a withdrawal over the counter. She then, out of the corner of her eye, became aware of someone staring into the phone box. "I won't be a minute," she called, as she turned to see who it was - and saw that it was herself looking into the telephone kiosk.

An ice-cold tingle spread over her scalp, and her stomach churned. Her exact double - same hair, same face - but definitely not her reflection, was standing there smiling. Jaclyn dropped the telephone handset and pushed the door of the kiosk open. She ran off towards Myrtle Street and did not stop running until she reached Sugnall Street, at the back of the Philharmonic Hall. She then looked back for the first time, only to see her eerie carbon-copy following at a distance of about forty metres, and so she ran on again, panic-stricken, over Hope Street and down Hardman Street. She hesitated at the junction of Pilgrim Street, and considered running down there, but thought it wise to keep to the main thoroughfare, where plenty of people were about.

The whole thing was like a nightmare, and she somehow doubted the reality of what was happening, whilst responding to it unquestioningly. She ran as fast as she could down Leece Street and looked back as she passed the bombed-out church of St Luke's, only to see the sinister twin jogging along after her.

An uncharacteristically violent thought suddenly entered Jaclyn's head: get a knife, or even a hatchet from the hardware store on Renshaw Street, then confront the look-alike and stab her, or hack her to bits. The aggressive notions were born out of sheer terror. Why isn't there ever a policeman about when you need one? Jaclyn wondered, and she started to gasp for breath. Just five years ago she would have been fit enough to race away from this unearthly danger, but half a decade of cigarettes and the wrong food had taken its toll. The sharp pain of a stitch in her side slowed her down as she reached the pedestrian crossing on Berry Street.

She was fit to drop from exhaustion by the time she reached Bold Street, and she sought refuge in a newsagents. People in the shop stared at her, and some undoubtedly assumed the worst; that she was on the run from the police, perhaps. Jaclyn waited near the shop counter, gazing intently at the front windows, expecting to see her replica appear at any minute, but it didn't. All the same, Jaclyn hung about for as long as possible, until she felt brave enough and sufficiently recovered to leave the Bold Street shop.

She then made her way to her bank on Lord Street, checking over her shoulder all the time. She notified the cashier about the loss of her debit and credit cards and filled in the necessary forms, and then made a withdrawal of one hundred pounds. She took a taxi to Claire's home in Huyton, only to find that her friend was in town shopping. How ironic! Claire's forty-year-old brother Sam told her to wait, as he expected his sister to be back at noon, as she had agreed to mind his four-year-old daughter. Jaclyn did not dare tell Sam about the shocking double of herself that had stalked her, as she knew he would think she was losing her marbles. Claire arrived home at around twenty minutes past noon, and at first she behaved coldly towards Jaclyn, until her friend threw her arms around her and made a profuse apology. Claire hugged her back, and the two women went off to talk in private in the kitchen, as Sam went down the road to fetch his daughter. Since the night before, Claire had discovered that 'Craig' - most probably an assumed name - was a young confidence trickster, whose speciality was robbing from vulnerable women who had had a little too much to drink. Claire had also heard that part of his *modus operandi* was to stage a fake fight with his partner in crime, to act as a distraction when a robbery had taken place. Jaclyn now knew, without a doubt, that Craig had stolen her purse and mobile, but that was really of no concern now, compared to the weird event which had taken place that morning. When she told Claire what had happened, her friend looked at her under heavy lids and asked, "Are you sure your drink wasn't spiked last night?"

"I'm positive it wasn't!" said Jaclyn in a raised voice. "I knew you wouldn't believe me, and I don't blame you, in a way, but I swear on my kid brother's life this happened. I was scared stiff."

"Okay, go through it one more time," said Claire, grabbing Jaclyn's hand and squeezing it, and this time she took in all the details of the story.

"What's going on?" Jaclyn asked, her eyebrows tilting inwards in consternation.

"Jackie, I don't know, but I believe you," Claire told her, then as an afterthought, she added, "but don't say anything about this to Sam - he'll think you're mad."

Jaclyn stayed with Claire till 5pm that afternoon, when Sam returned to pick up his daughter. Claire then went to Canning Street with her friend and stayed with her in the flat for nearly two hours. She gave Jaclyn her old mobile phone, and then they debated the existence of the 'doppelganger'. "Maybe it was just someone who had a strong resemblance to you - they say everyone has a double, you know," was Claire's rather lame take on the odd incident.

Jaclyn shook her head and dismissed that theory with a grimace. "A double with the exact same clothes on as me? No way. I think it's some sort of omen - I really do."

Claire tried to reassure her friend that it was not an omen and that there was probably a perfectly natural explanation, but Jaclyn had deep misgivings about the experience. Jaclyn's bullying husband then became the topic of conversation, and not for the first time, either. Claire said he had been spotted with a young woman on his arm in a Mathew Street pub. "Mmm, she won't be on his arm for long when she finds out what he's really like,' said Jaclyn through gritted teeth. "I feel sorry for her."

After Claire had gone home, Jaclyn sat on the sofa watching a film on her portable television set. She tried to drive the whole surreal episode of the double from her mind, and at midnight, Claire telephoned to see if she was okay. Jaclyn said she was fine, and not long afterwards, she went to bed. She sat up with her back resting against two propped-up eiderdown pillows as she struggled to read one of the most clichéd 'chick-lit' books she had ever come across. At around a quarter to one, she almost vomited with fear as her double appeared once again - standing inside the full-length mirror of the wardrobe. The acidic reflux from Jaclyn's stomach into her throat almost choked her.

The perfect imitation of herself stepped out of the wardrobe mirror and advanced slowly towards her, still wearing the same clothes it had worn during the previous encounter. Jaclyn coughed and spluttered, as vile stomach acid stung her oesophagus, and she scrambled across the duvet, taking refuge on the other side of the bed. Her eyes scanned the room frantically for a weapon, but she could only find a narrow brass magazine rack box. She picked it up and hurled it at the clone-like figure, which was now circling around the bottom of the bed, closing in on her with an evil smile on its face. The rack missed its intended target, striking a cabinet across the room instead.

When Jaclyn's spitting image was about six feet away, it raised its hands in a threatening manner, as if it intended to strangle her right there and then. Jaclyn seized an old upright chair and thrust its legs into the chest and abdomen of her alter ego. The twin let out a gruff winded sound and toppled backwards from the impact. It soon got up again though, and as Jaclyn raised the chair, intending to smash it down on her spine-chilling three-dimensional mirror image, the figure charged at her with lightning agility. The chair smashed down on the carpet, as the dead ringer seized Jaclyn by the throat. Its cold, emotionless eyes met the terrified eyes of its prey and it started to choke Jaclyn with a rapidly tightening two-hand grip.

"No!" Jaclyn gasped, as she was pinned up against the wall.

"I'm taking your life," the flesh and blood duplicate gloated, "because you don't deserve it."

"Why?" Jaclyn croaked, sensing death was only seconds away. She tried to unlock the double's arms but they were like cast-iron and would not budge. "You're the weak one, and I'm the other side of you!" the second Jaclyn announced. The psychopath of supernatural origin grinned broadly, obviously enjoying terrorising his victim.

Jaclyn thrust her hands up on to the strangler's face, and placed her thumbs over those wicked blue eyes. She pressed the eyeballs in with all of her remaining strength, digging her nails into them as she did so, and as they burst and sprayed pale watery liquid all over her, the head of her counterpart seemed to deflate like a punctured balloon. The throttling hands loosened their grip and the body silently slithered to the floor and seemed to disintegrate into cloth. Jaclyn flew to the door, fighting for breath, wheezing and howling. She pressed the light switch, and felt something slippery and wet under her right thumb. She shuddered at the sudden realisation of what it was - the vile milky fluid from one of the popped eyeballs.

She then gingerly crept around the bed to see what was left of that 'thing'. In the bright illumination of the neon light-fitting, a stringy grey heap of something resembling a spider's cobweb lay on the floor where the double had fallen. She telephoned Claire and begged her to come around to the flat. She gave her a garbled version of what had happened, and kept coughing, as though her throat had been injured from the half-throttling she had received just minutes ago. Claire told Jaclyn she would phone her brother Sam and ask him to collect her, but Jaclyn said she didn't want that; she wanted Claire to come and see something for herself at the Canning Street flat. Claire said she would visit in the morning but Jaclyn kept on imploring her to come to the flat immediately.

Claire eventually caved in and agreed to visit her troublesome friend at 1.30am - just what she needed after a hard night's work! As soon as Jaclyn answered the front door of the flat, Claire started grumbling about the cost of the taxi fare and said she could not visit like this again, but then she noticed the extensive bruises on Jaclyn's neck, left by the double's cruel hands. Jaclyn ran up the stairs to the first-floor flat saying, "Hurry up, quick, Claire! I want you to see something."

Claire followed, and as soon as she entered the flat, Jaclyn ushered her straight into the bedroom. "Look at this! Look, here's proof!" and she pointed to the bundle of silky cobweb-like material lying at the side of the bed.

"What is it?" Claire asked, and she crouched down to get a better look.

Jaclyn gave an account of the terrifying confrontation with the facsimile, then carefully picked up a piece of the substance using the tip of a ballpoint pen. The greyish, translucent material looked like a type of adhesive gauze, and it reconstituted itself into a shadowy and transparent replica of a hand as Jaclyn lifted the pen. "Ugh! Chuck it out, Jackie," said Claire, her face contorted in disgust at the repulsive-looking stuff. Jaclyn carefully picked up another piece of her double's wispy residue with the pen and shuddered as she recognised what looked like the shed skin of a familiar upturned nose in sheer-woven fabric.

Jaclyn had no intention of throwing the substance away - it was her only evidence, after all - and went to get a spatula from the kitchen. She told Claire that she intended to store the doppelganger's 'skin' in a jar and take it to be analysed at Liverpool University, but by the time Jaclyn had found a suitable jar and emptied it of its biscuits, the unnatural residual traces of her double had vanished.

A material called 'Angel's hair' - which often falls from the sky after the materialisation and dematerialisation of UFOs, has been known to behave in a similar, tantalising way. It too resembles a filamentous substance that evaporates into nothing, even when it has been successfully transferred into sealed jars. Ectoplasm, that fabled substance which is said to be excreted by mediums during séances, is also said to fade away within a short space of time, possibly back into its own dimension.

Jaclyn saw her menacing doppelganger no more after that eventful morning, but she was haunted by the words it had said. She wondered what it had meant when it had told her that she didn't deserve her life, and also when it had said, "You're the weak one, and I'm the other side of you!" She pondered long and hard over those few words and suspected that the malevolent double represented the tough side to her personality; a side that had never really seen the light of day, especially in recent years. It didn't take much soul-searching for Jaclyn to realise that she was an overly submissive type, always being walked over by someone, especially her husband, and yet when she drank, the flip side of her personality - a Jaclyn who stood up for herself- had come to the fore.

A month after the doppelganger incident, Jaclyn had been drinking with Claire in a city centre club one night, when she bumped into her estranged husband Chris. He told her she was coming home with him in his usual macho manner, in front of a few drinking buddies, but Jaclyn stood her ground and said she was not going anywhere with him. And when he tried to grab her arm, Jaclyn turned around and delivered a sharp upper-cut to his jaw, which knocked him out cold. Chris's friends stood there in awe, as the eighteen-stone Chris fell on to his back and remained there with his eyes half open. As she punched Chris, Jaclyn saw the eyes of that doppelganger, close up, as they had looked that morning when she was being choked.

I interviewed Jaclyn several times, and also Claire, and I have many similar doppelganger cases on file. It is strange how, when people 'act out of character' they often say things like, "I wasn't myself when I did that," or "I don't know what came over me" and "I don't know what possessed me".

Perhaps there is a Mr Hyde deep down in all of us, just waiting for a chance to burst out...

HILTY

Occasionally a story comes my way on which I cannot throw any light whatsoever. Such tales seem to defy all explanation, and despite my many years spent studying the paranormal, I am at a loss to rationalise them. The following story certainly falls into this category. Perhaps you can fathom it out?

It all started when eleven-year-old John Murphy and his six-year-old sister Mary visited their Aunty Frances, an oddball of a woman with peculiar behaviour patterns, who lived off Heyworth Street, in Everton. The only reason they were paying the visit was in the hope of getting a few bob for sweets, because Frances, as barmy as she was, was a generous person whenever she had money, especially to her nephews and nieces.

On this particular windy Saturday afternoon in March 1965, Frances left her eight-month-old baby, Jim, in his cot in the parlour and then said she was just popping out to have a word with Mrs Winneral, who lived about thirty yards down the road. She wouldn't be long she said, and warned little "Meddlesome Mary" not to disturb the baby's sleep. "I'll be back soon, Carrot Cake," she then said to John, insensitive to the fact that he hated that nickname, referring as it did to his mop of bright red hair.

Mary had brought her little plastic baby doll Miranda with her to the house, and she tried to shove it into the cot, on top of little Jim, who was fast asleep.

"Stop that, Mary," John warned her. "You'll wake the baby and then Aunt Frances won't get us any sweets."

"I won't!" shouted Mary, standing on a chair so she could get a proper view of Jim.

"Be quiet will you? She told you not to wake the baby," and John snatched the doll off his little sister.

"Give me that back - now!" shrieked Mary, her nostrils flared and her little eyes bulging with annoyance.

Just then a tiny mongrel dog ran into the house. It sounds like a far-fetched cliché to our ears in these times of sky-high crime rates, but in those days, you really could leave your front door open, and sometimes - on rare occasions -cats or dogs would stroll into your home off the street. This scruffy little canine specimen had a loveable face with large expressive eyes. Mary fell in love with him right away and picked him up and began to fuss over him, but he barked in protest and sprang from her over-enthusiastic rib-cracking embrace and scampered into the kitchen, where he began sniffing the air as the meaty aroma from a pan of stew simmering on the stove reached his nostrils.

John used a fork to skewer a piece of partly-boiled stewing steak from the pan, then blew on it until it was lukewarm. The dog sat on its hind legs in a begging posture, whining in anticipation of the treat he was about to receive. Mary giggled and asked if she could feed the dog the morsel. "No you can't," replied John, and he dropped the piece of meat for the dog, whose little jaw opened with perfect timing and caught the food mid-air. The animal had very muddy paws and

Mary suggested they should wash him, so John fetched a washtub from the yard and put it down on the kitchen floor. He filled a copper kettle to full capacity and put it on the gas ring and then found some newspaper, and tore a strip off to screw up into a taper. He used the flame under the pan of stew to light the other gas ring and put the kettle on it.

Somewhere along the line, John put the washtub on the ancient gas cooker and took the pan of stew off the boil to give himself more room to directly boil the water in the washtub. Mary stood on a stool, with a ladle in her hand, scooping water from a running tap into the washtub. Two fierce rings of flame licked the underside of the galvanised tub. The plan was to dunk the dog in the warm tub and give him a good wash, but the furry little scavenger, suspecting something of the sort, had escaped back the way he had come.

Meanwhile, Aunty Frances was still busy gossiping with Mrs Winneral and the two women had recently been joined by gossiper extraordinaire, Mrs Huggins. Now Frances Murphy was a little afraid to leave, in case Mrs Winneral and Mrs Huggins started talking about her the minute her back was turned. Left to his own devices, John decided to go and have a mooch around upstairs in the bedrooms, and when he came down just five minutes later, he found Mary hysterical, and in tears. "A man took the baby!" she screamed, and pointed down the hall, towards the kitchen. There were ominous boiling and bubbling sounds coming from the kitchen, and steam had settled on the vestibule door's pane of glass and was even trickling down the walls. John felt butterflies in his stomach. "Where did this man go?" he cried.

"In - the - kitchen!" Mary managed to tell him between convulsive sobs. She was so distressed she almost made herself sick.

John walked into the kitchen and his heart sank when he saw that the door leading to the backyard was standing ajar. The water he and Mary had left in the bathtub was now boiling furiously, and in it lay a baby bobbing about in the bubbling reddish water. John turned around and ran past Mary, heading for the front parlour. The cot was empty, just as she had said. His heart somersaulted. The baby had been boiled alive by a madman.

Mary tried to grab at John as he ran out of the house, but he was too quick. She watched him run down the street and vanish around a corner. "John!" the little girl screamed, "Come back, John," and she rubbed her red swollen eyes of stinging tears with the sleeves of her jersey.

John fled down Heyworth Street, and almost tripped over the old arthritic dog that was always to be found sitting on the pavement outside the premises of Fletchers the Butchers. An elderly man who knew John's father came out of Bolams the Barbers, wiping the nape of his neck with a handkerchief. He could see that the lad looked terrified, and tried to stop him to ask what the matter was but John dodged him and ran blindly across the road. A hackney cab sounded its horn after screeching to a halt, missing the running boy by inches.

John Murphy aimlessly wandered the grey streets of Liverpool, trying to drive that sickening image of the boiling baby from his mind. Why was he even on the run? He had not been responsible, but he was terrified of facing the formidable Aunt Frances. She was unpredictable at the best of times, so who knows how she might react on finding that her baby had been boiled alive. She had left the baby in his care, after all. What would she do when she found little Jim all red raw, and as soggy as an over-cooked cauliflower? She would have found out by now, John reflected with a tear being blown across his cheek by the fierce March wind. Another depressing thought then entered his troubled mind; what if the police did not believe Mary's story about the intruder putting Jim in the tub? Then they would think it was him that had done it, and how could he disprove it?

Downcast and in deep thought, he passed a pub called the Clock Inn, on William Henry Street, as a thick dark cloud killed what little sunlight remained of the dying day. As he was passing an alleyway, a grubby hand shot out and grabbed him by the collar, and for one nasty moment, John thought it was a policeman's hand. "Come 'ere, you!" said a young gruff voice. The voice belonged to a thickset lad, a little older perhaps than John, and a little taller than him too. He looked tough with his shaved head, and a pair of wonky NHS spectacles balanced on his nose, with a plaster covering one of the lenses.

"Get off," John tried to remove the rough's hand from his collar but the bespectacled bully clenched his other hand and made a fist at the runaway. "Yer're coming with me, carrot-top," the skinhead announced, and he dragged John down the alleyway.

"My mum's only just round the corner," fibbed John, but the tough guy with the lazy eye knew he was lying and told him to shut up.

"I want yer to do somethin' for me, and then maybe yer can go." The delinquent, whose name was Jack, let go of John's collar at the other end of the alleyway and pointed to some unattended roadworks nearby. "Get them lanterns for me - both of 'em. If yer don't, and yer run away, I'll come after yer and batter yer."

John looked at the two unlit red paraffin-fuelled danger lights situated next to a hole in the road. "Alright, I'll get them. And then do you promise I can go?" he asked in a quavering voice.

"Hurry up!" the young tyrant ordered, and pushed John out into the street. John sneaked up to the tall striped tent that a watchman would usually sit in at night. He peeped from behind it at two women who were chatting about fifty yards away. When he was sure they were not watching him, he walked out from behind the tent as nonchalantly as he could and picked the lamps up by their U-shaped handle strips, and then walked back to the instigator of the theft, who was peeping out from the alleyway.

"That's it!" said the young yob, and was pushing John back down the alleyway until suddenly he started tugging on the back of his coat. "Hang on," he said, and pushed open the old flaking door to one of the backyards and shoved him inside. His tormentor followed and bolted the door after them both. They crossed a small yard full of tall purple-headed weeds sprouting from the cracks in the uneven paving. A few loose bricks from the half-collapsed neighbouring wall lay scattered here and there.

The strong-armed child opened what had once been the door to a back kitchen in an old derelict house on William Henry Street. Most of the windows were barricaded with sheets of corrugated iron, and the houses on each side were also empty, and scheduled for demolition in the near future. In the immediate space inside the kitchen, the unknown hard-knock took out a lighter and lit the wicks of the newly acquired roadworks lamps. He then closed the door behind himself and John, and gravely issued a set of curious instructions, whilst keeping a very serious expression on his face that seemed in advance of his age. "Stay right behind me, and do exactly as I say."

He walked forward holding aloft the two lamps, which only gave off a feeble red light, through the kitchen, and into a long dark passageway. There must have been over a hundred square razor blades embedded in the walls on each side of that narrow passageway and John Murphy stared in fear at those walls, wondering what sort of maniac would do such a dangerous thing as planting blades in them.

"There's a wire 'ere, step over it carefully," instructed the weird hoodlum. A thin but highly dangerous length of piano wire, sharp as cheese-cutter wire, had been strung across their path at calf level. Both children stepped over it with the utmost care and then, about four feet down the razor-walled passageway, there was another thin piano wire strung horizontally from wall to wall at neck level. They both had to duck to avoid it. Anyone running into this wire would risk serious injury, if not partial decapitation.

At last they reached a huge room with a bunch of candles burning on a dusty old table. The place was filled with a strong smell of dirt, damp and decay.

"Alright, my name's Jack," said the menacing boy, placing the red lamps on the table. "What's your name?"

"John Murphy, but why have you brought me here? I want to go home." John was extremely upset, and imagined that Jack was going to kill him, or do something unspeakably evil to him.

"If I show you a secret, d'yer cross yer heart and hope to die?" asked Jack.

"Yes, I cross my heart." John traced a cross on his chest with his index and middle finger. "And then can I go?"

"If he says yer can, yer can."

"Who do you mean?" John asked, looking around nervously for his accomplice.

Instead of answering, Jack pitched another strange question at the poor lad, "Who d'yer love most in all the world?" he asked.

There was a pause as John thought about the question for a moment. The March winds outside whistled and howled through the cracks in the windows and floors of the old ruined house. "My mum," he finally replied. Jack did not acknowledge his reply but instead just pitched another strange question at him.

"If yer tell anyone about what yer see in here, yer mum'll have a really horrible death, have yer got that?" As he delivered this threat, Jack's top lip curled up with an expression of pure hatred. "Y - y - yes."

John's knees felt as if they were about to buckle under him. What was the secret Jack was going to reveal? Had he killed someone in here? Was that what the stomach-churning smell of decay was all about?

"Hilty? Are you there?" Jack suddenly enquired, seeming to address the darkness, his one visible eye swivelling as he turned, as if he were looking for something on the dilapidated walls. All John could see was peeling old wallpaper and holes in the wall where crumbling plasterboard showed through. He did notice a long thin black gap in the wall facing him, and that gap suddenly moved. In fact it turned out not to be a gap at all - it was something which struck John Murphy dumb with heart-stopping terror.

A enormously tall figure, easily over seven feet in height, stepped out from the wall. It had a pointed, teardrop-shaped head, and wore what looked like a black balaclava, through which a very sinister white face was showing. That face was almost triangular in shape, with a pointed chin. The lips of the oddly smiling mouth were jet black, and the teeth looked red, as if they had - as if they had blood on them. The eyes were ringed with heavy black borders and were pink with tiny dark pupils. The clothing this weird figure wore was close-fitting and black, and the shoes were very long and pointed. A sweet sickly smell, which seemed to be a mixture of lavender and decomposition, suddenly pervaded the room.

John felt goose pimples rising on his arms, legs and especially the back of his neck. He was so afraid he thought his pounding heart would explode out of his chest. The figure spoke in a high-pitched effeminate voice. "What have you brought me this time, Jack? Red hair is it? He must be descended from some bastard of a Dane."

The tall entity in black reached out an impossibly long skinny arm and a black gloved hand with abnormally long fingers extended out to John's face, but the boy suddenly found himself turning away and running for the passageway.

The unearthly thing's mood changed in a flash and it let out a terrifying high-pitched shriek. Even in his panic, John remembered the piano wire and slowed down and felt for it with a trembling hand. He deftly ducked under the wire as he heard thudding footsteps closing in behind him. He ran a few more feet and then stopped and felt the air for the second piano wire with the sole of his shoe, and having located it, then hopped over it, all the time aware that Jack was hot on his heels.

Having reached the end of the lethal passageway and run across the kitchen, John pulled the door open and ran across the neglected backyard, through the tangle of weeds, to the back gate. Jack came tearing out of the kitchen doorway, but as he did so, John bent down and picked up one of the loose bricks from the crumbling wall. With both hands he hurled it with all his might at Jack's face. There was a sickening dull thud, and Jack toppled backwards and lay groaning amongst the weeds. John quickly undid the bolt of the backyard door and tore off down the alleyway.

When he got back on to William Henry Street it was deserted, and it was only then that he regained the power of speech. He screamed out for help until he thought his lungs would burst. Suddenly, one of the corrugated sheets covering one of the front windows of the empty house on the street was rammed forward by someone inside the derelict premises - someone with substantial strength, in fact. A long black arm was thrust out from the gap behind the sheet, and once again those long tapering fingers and thumb tried to grab at John Murphy. It managed to seize his coat, and the high-pitched voice inside the house emitted a string of obscene swear words, as the thing cursed the escapee. John fled, abandoning his coat to the entity's clutches. He did not stop running until he was a great distance away and he was amongst people once again.

The heavens opened and he went the rest of his way home without his coat in a downpour, and when he reached his house he hammered as loudly as he could on the knocker, still nervously glancing behind himself, expecting that skinny devil in black to come haring down the road at any minute.

John's mother answered the door and after scolding her son because he had gone out "gallivanting" without telling anyone where he had vanished to, Mrs Murphy hugged him and they went into the house together, where Mary was sitting watching television and Mr Murphy was snoring in his armchair under the pages of the Football Echo, which were vibrating in a comical manner. As Mrs Murphy dried off her son in front of the fire, he rattled off his strange account of that day's extraordinary happenings, but she was only half listening and just put it down to childish prattle. However, on the following morning, when Mrs Murphy and her son went in search of his new coat, they found it torn to shreds and draped over the railings in front of the house on William Henry Street.

It transpired that the "strange man" who had taken the baby that Saturday afternoon had been Mrs Winneral's brother Desmond. He had collected the baby and taken it to its mother, Frances, on Mrs Winneral's instructions, just so she could prolong their gossiping session. Desmond was said (in those times) to be "a bit slow". He had gone out of Aunt Frances's house through the backyard door and into the entry. The baby in the boiling bath had, of course, been Miranda, Mary's doll, which the little girl had accidentally dropped into the tub. The redness of the bubbling water was the scarlet dye running from the doll's clothes.

As you can imagine, John Murphy was mightily relieved to learn all this, but he had terrible nightmares about Hilty for years afterwards. Even though John told his mum what had happened, Jack's dire promise of Mrs Murphy suffering a horrible death never came to pass, nor did anything fatal ever happen to John for telling his mum about the uncanny figure in the 'bombdie' - Sixties slang for a dilapidated and deserted house.

A few years after hearing about this bizarre series of events, I received a telephone call one day at the offices of Radio Merseyside after talking about ghosts in the Everton area whilst on air. An elderly woman, a Mrs Kelly, rang in and said something that really gave me a jolt. She asked me if I had ever heard of the weird ghost in black who had haunted a house on William Henry Street in the late 1950s. The children described this ghost as a tall man in black with a pointed hat, and used to call him the 'Gilly-Gilly Man'. This bears no resemblance to the name 'Hilty', of course - which is what John had heard Jack call the entity, but what was striking was the description of what must surely be the same entity.

Mrs Kelly said the Gilly-Gilly Man was said to live in the cellar of the empty house on William Henry Street, and he also roamed the city's sewers. Mrs Kelly's mother would often tell her not to talk behind anyone's back, because Gilly-Gilly was listening through plugholes in the bath and also through pipes and keyholes, and he would pass on the bad things he gleaned in this way, to the people spoken about. The mental picture of the ghost eavesdropping in such a way must have frightened children, just as the stories of Spring-Heeled Jack had fifty years before. Who, or what, was the entity that haunted that house on William Henry Street? Was it some evil spirit, or a demon perhaps? Or, was it something from some other dimension or parallel world? At the moment, until I get more information on Hilty, I simply do not know.

Note: just after I had committed this story to the page, something very odd took place. The door to my study opened all by itself until it was wide open, and I saw a long shadow in the hallway but nothing visible was casting that shadow. A moment later the door closed again on its own. I have an uneasy feeling that I might have stirred up Hilty by committing his story to the page.

THE LITTLE OLD LADY

The following tale is the result of a taped interview with a Mrs Gallagher of Old Swan; a separate, and apparently unrelated account of a ghost on Edge Lane given by John Crawford; and many hours of research in the Public Record Office in the Central Library on William Brown Street.

Back in the 1980s, long before the advent of PlayStations and X Boxes, there were one or two exciting 'video game' arcades in the city centre, where teenaged children hung out. One arcade stood on London Road and another was to be found on Skelhorne Street, but the one to be featured in this peculiar story, stood around the corner on Lime Street, where you could play coin-operated games such as Lunar Lander, Missile Command, Defender, Donkey Kong, Pacman, Asteroids and other electronic escapes from a dreary city that was being devastated by recession.

This incident took place on Saturday, 7 July 1984. On that day, things were looking bleak for Britain - and all of western civilisation, come to think of it. The then deeply-Conservative magazine, *The Economist*, was joining the growing ranks of public opinion criticising Mrs Thatcher and her cabinet, with an editorial claiming that the Government was becoming the most inept administration since the war.

The security of the world was also in the news that day, when the Kremlin chiefs strongly criticised the United States for militarising space. President Reagan's administration was going ahead with the so-called 'Star Wars' military programme - the Strategic Defence Initiative. Up to this point in history, the USA and the USSR had both accumulated enough nuclear weaponry to annihilate one another - the so-called Mutually Assured Destruction (M.A.D.) doctrine - and this had served as a deterrent to World War III for decades. M.A.D. assured there would be no winners in a nuclear conflict, as both sides would be wiped out, leaving the world to crumble into a radioactive hell of firestorms, carcinogenic fall-out and grotesque mutations, in a formidable nuclear winter.

President Reagan wanted high-powered beam weapons, space-based missiles and orbiting 'hypervelocity railguns' (capable of shooting small projectiles at twenty-four miles per second) to intercept and blast any incoming Russian inter-continental ballistic missiles (ICBMs) to smithereens, should they be fired at the Unites States and other NATO countries.

That Saturday, as the country sank ever deeper into economic depression, and the world tottered on the brink of nuclear destruction, some people sought escape from the gloom and doom in the most unlikely of distractions, such as the television coverage of the Wimbledon Finals on *Grandstand*, and fifty-five-year-old Eric Johnson was one of these escapists. He reclined in his deckchair in the back-garden of his Dovecot home, sipping from a can of iced Guinness as he enjoyed the Ladies' Doubles on his portable television. The only cloud on the horizon was Andrew, Eric's fourteen-year-old son. He looked ripe for committing mischief, snooping over the fence into his neighbour's back garden. Then he vanished for a while - always a bad sign, thought the lad's father - and Eric finally snapped when he noticed the thin barrel of an air rifle protruding from the bathroom window upstairs.

"Andy! What're you playing at?" Eric bawled, and as his bulky frame vacated the deckchair with some difficulty, the air rifle barrel was quickly withdrawn and the sound of mumbled cursing could be heard coming from the bathroom. The weapon - on loan from 'Rambo' McKay, the seventeen-year-old scourge of the neighbourhood, who lived three doors away - was immediately confiscated by an exasperated Eric. "Here you are - now get lost!" he said, in an act of unprecedented generosity, as he slapped a ten-pound note into his son's hand. "God! It comes to something when you have to pay just to get a bit of peace and quiet." Without even saying thank you, Andrew was, within five minutes, on the bus bound for the Lime Street arcade, to blow his unexpected windfall.

Eric settled back in his deckchair and was just catching up on the state of play, when he shot up, cursing to himself. He had just remembered that today was his wife's forty-seventh birthday and he had completely forgotten all about it. Now he would have to go and buy her a card and a present. What a nuisance!

Within the hour, Andrew's ten pounds had been gobbled up by the games machines, but he had gained two new friends at the arcade: 'Franno' - a tall gangly streetwise Toxteth teenager of about thirteen, and 'Match' - a quiet scrawny little scheming type from Old Swan, who had earned his nickname because he always carried matches, and loved to set fire to things. Andrew judged him to be a little bit older than himself. The teenaged trio left the arcade and walked up Copperas Hill. Franno spotted a maroon Audi GTS parked in a secluded part of Greek Street. "Bet yer I could break into that car in five seconds," he bragged.

"Go on then, I'll keep Dixie," said Match.

"There's a cop shop just there - look!" said Andrew and nodded towards Copperas Hill Police Station, which stood about twenty yards away.

"Better leave it then," said Franno walking on and stroking the Audi's wing mirror as he passed.

"You're all talk, you," Match told Franno. "Yer make out yer can rob things and that, but you're dead scared of bein' caught."

"Shurrup, Match," mumbled Franno, irritated, pretending to be looking up at something in the clear blue sky.

Andrew suddenly recalled the black sheep of his extended family, Tony, and seized the opportunity to impress his new mates. "My cousin Tony's in Hindley Prison. He's really hard, my cousin."

"Hindley isn't a prison, yer liar, it's a youth custody centre," said Franno, and he spat through the gap in his front teeth and started to fantasise. "I was in Hindley for twelve months. I've been in Walton as well, for bank robbery."

Match sprang into action and challenged Franno's ludicrous claim. "Swear on your Michael's life then. Swear on his life - that you went to Walton Gaol!" "I don't have to," Franno replied, looking hurt because Match had challenged him and tried to humiliate him in front of a stranger.

The three teenagers strolled up Pembroke Place and along Irvine Street, and ten minutes later they were to be found in Wavertree Park, larking about on the swings and throwing dry sods of earth at passersby and people walking their dogs. After a while they grew bored and wandered off to Match's home on St Oswald Street, where they drank cheap cider and wolfed down bags of crisps in his bedroom. The lads became so noisy, singing and messing about, that Match's mum soon turfed them back out.

By 9pm the three urban adventurers were walking up Edge Lane, when Match noticed something which immediately caught his attention - an empty terraced house with no curtains on its bay windows, and when Match pressed his nose up against the glass, he could see a small tin box lying on the floor in the front room. What was in the box? Match just had to find out, and so he convinced his two friends to help him break into the house.

In the fading summer twilight, the three young rogues sneaked down the alleyway which ran behind the row of houses, and came to a backyard door that bore the white painted number of the empty house. The back gate was locked, so the boys scaled the yard wall, and once in the yard, Match found the way to get inside, by breaking a pane in the back parlour window with a brick wrapped in his coat to muffle the sound. He then reached through the hole in the smashed window pane and undid the catch, which was stiff with rust.

The three of them climbed through the window and set about exploring the back parlour. There was nothing there but bare floorboards and old broadsheet newspapers strewn about everywhere. Match tightly screwed up a bunch of these papers and with the matches he always carried, he lit a torch of flame. Meanwhile, Franno had crawled into the front parlour from the hallway, keeping low so that no one passing by would see him, and grabbed the tin box. He shook it gently and held it to his ear - there was definitely something in it. He scuttled back into the back parlour to find out what was in the tin.

It turned out to be a large old-fashioned brooch, studded with dark shiny stones, which Franno promptly threw on the floor - and a bundle of old receipts, birthday cards, and other boring documents. They were also discarded and thrown on the floor. Andrew Johnson thought the brooch might be worth something and so he picked it up and pocketed it. Following Match's example, Franno then twisted a few newspaper pages from the floor into a huge taper, and ignited it from the flames of Match's torch. He then went into the hall and climbed the stairs to see if there was anything more interesting in the bedrooms. Less than half a minute later he came bounding back down.

"There's somethin' up there!" he cried, nearly knocking Match flying as he came careering back into the back parlour.

"Will yer be quiet?" said Match in a loud whisper. "Yer'll get us all caught if yer not careful!"

Then Andrew and Match heard high-pitched yelps coming from upstairs and light footsteps, like a child's, coming down the stairs. Within seconds, all three teenagers were tearing across the backyard. In one mad acrobatic sprint, Franno ran up the backyard wall and managed to grab the top and haul himself over it. Match was next, closely followed by Andrew, who, when he was atop the wall, looked back and thought he saw a tiny pale face, gazing out of the smashed back parlour window. He dropped down into the alleyway and ran off as fast as his legs could carry him to Rathbone Road.

Match set off for his home in Old Swan, after agreeing to meet up with his two new friends in the Lime Street arcade some other time. Franno and Andrew then quizzed each other about what they had just seen or heard in the empty Edge Lane house. Franno said he had seen a "weird-looking kid" in one of the upstairs rooms, and Andrew described how he had thought he had seen a child's face peeping out at him from the back parlour window, but neither could explain how a child had come to be in the empty house on his own. Franno's bravado had been severely tested by what he had seen and it was clear that he had had a real fright. He parted ways with Andrew at the junction of Picton Road and Wellington Road, and headed southwards to his home in Toxteth.

Andrew didn't have any money left to get the bus

home, so he walked all the way from Wavertree High Street to his home in Pilch Lane, Dovecot, which took nearly forty minutes because he was not too familiar with the streets of Wavertree and parts of Childwall. It might have been nothing more than his imagination, stirred up by the uncanny events at the Edge Lane house, but throughout the journey home through the night streets, he felt as if someone was following him. More than once he heard faint footsteps trailing behind him, but when he turned round there was never anyone there. He also thought he heard a faint whining voice on two occasions, but again there was no one behind him.

At around 10.20pm, Andrew finally arrived back home and his anxious mother, Carol Johnson, asked where he had been. He was just about to tell her about the evenings spooky goings on at the empty house, but stopped himself just in time when he remembered that he had actually broken into that house; something he still could not quite believe. Instead, he lied and said he had been over at his mate Kevin's house, on Adcote Road.

When Andrew walked into the living room he immediately noticed the single birthday card standing forlornly on the sideboard. He picked it up and recognised his father's appallingly wonky block-letter handwriting inside. "Is it your birthday today, Mum?" he asked, with genuine concern. He had always bought his mother something for her birthday - how could have forgotten this time?

"Yeah, it is," Carol told him with a slight smile and shake of the head and without taking her eyes away from the television screen. Eric, meanwhile, was stretched out on the sofa, snoring.

"I'm sorry, Mum, I'll get you something really nice tomorrow. I clean forgot it was your birthday."

"Tomorrow's Sunday, love," she replied. "But it's alright anyway, I'd rather forget birthdays at my age. Are you hungry? Have you had anything to eat tonight?"

"No, I'm starving, Mum. I haven't had anything since lunchtime."

Andrew delved into his pocket and took a quick look at the brooch from the tin box in that empty house. He was still looking at it, halfway up the stairs when his mother popped her head out of the kitchen doorway and called up that she was going to warm his tea up in the oven. Andrew just nodded and then hurried on up to his bedroom, where he was able to have a good look at the brooch for the first time. It was silver by the looks of it, with three large cushion-set amethyst stones. He wondered if he should give it to his mother as a birthday present; it did look old and valuable, but was it her kind of thing? And would she start asking awkward questions about where he had got it from? As he was mulling all this over there was a heavy knock on the front door, making Andrew jump. What if it was the police? Maybe someone had been living in that empty-looking house after all. He quickly stuffed the brooch into one of his Doc Marten boots in the corner, then crept out on to the landing and sneaked to the top of the stairs to get a good view of the front door. His mother answered the door, and Andrew was relieved to see that it was only their neighbour Mrs Jones from next door, but what she said was very bizarre. She claimed her husband Arthur had seen "some little lad, or maybe a girl" on the path leading to their house. The person was no ordinary child, or even a dwarf, and must have been some kind of freak, Mrs Jones reasoned, because he or she was only about two and a half to three feet tall, with a very tiny head.

"On our path?" Carol asked, with a concerned look on her face. "Are you sure, Mrs Jones? Nobody's knocked and we'd have heard because we've been in all evening."

"Yes, on your path and he, or she, or whatever it was, pointed to your door, and made this dreadful crying sound to my Arthur, and then it disappeared off over that way. Arthur said he wasn't sure because it was dark, but he thought it was wearing a dress, but it could have been wide trousers."

About ten minutes later, after having a good old chin wag about a range of subjects, Mrs Jones left and Andrew's mum closed the door and went back into the kitchen.

"Is my tea ready now?" Andrew called down. "I'm proper starving."

"Oh, that makes a change! It'll be ready in a couple of minutes - Mrs Jones kept me chatting with some talk about a kid pointing to our door or something. I don't really know what she was going on about."

Then came a scratching sound at the front door.

Andrew looked at his mother, and she looked back at him, apprehension etched across her face. She went to the door but stopped short of opening it. "Who is it?" she called as Andrew stood next to her, listening.

There was a faint, high-pitched whimpering sound coming from outside on the doorstep.

"I said, who is it?" Carol cried out to the unknown visitor, louder this time.

The letterbox in the front door was set rather low - about five inches from the floor, and the flap on this letterbox suddenly squeaked open, as if the late-night caller was about to post something. Andrew and his mother stepped backwards. Then a minuscule hand, like that of a child's doll, reached in. It looked artificial at first, but then the tiny fingers and thumb bent and flexed and groped around in search of something.

Carol Johnson let out a loud shriek, which woke her husband from his slumbers on the sofa. He came running into the hallway to see what was going on and almost collided with her as she backed away from the eerie searching hand.

"What the hell are you screaming for? It's not another stupid spider is it?" Eric asked, and his wife quickly filled him in with what Mrs Jones had said, as she pointed to the letterbox, but the hand was no longer visible.

"Mind out the way," said Eric, shoving Andrew aside with a sigh of exasperation and reaching for the front door. "You can't get a minute's peace in this house. First it's our Andrew with that Rambo's air rifle - and now all this bloody nonsense!"

"Don't!" screamed Carol. "Don't open it! You don't know what's on the other side. It could be dangerous."

Eric ignored her and opened the door anyway. Outside the path was clear and there was no one to be seen, either in the front garden, or anywhere in the road. Carol clung on to her son, trembling as the cool night air wafted in from the front garden.

Eric soon came back in, saying, "She's mad next

door, there's no one outside."

Before he had chance to shut the door, Andrew cried out, "Dad! Look! Out there!" and he pointed to the darkness beyond the doorway. His father and mother recoiled in horror.

A little old lady, just over two feet in height, popped out of a gap in the garden hedge like a cork from a bottle. She had a neat little grey bun perched on the top of her head, and her wizened wrinkled face looked evil and full of anger. Her eyes were perfectly round, black and shiny, and her nose was very long and pointed, and her tight little mouth seemed to be fixed in an upside down crescent. She wore a cream high-collared blouse and an ankle-length black dress, both so outdated they must have last been in fashion over a hundred years ago. She very pointedly held out her left palm as she approached the door, as if she was begging for something, and she was still emitting that awful whingeing sound that Andrew and his mother had heard before.

"Oh my God! What the hell is that?" Eric whispered under his breath, as he backed away from the door.

Carol was more quick thinking and lunged towards the door and slammed it shut in the miniature old woman's face, but the letterbox flap quickly opened once more and the old woman's hand reached in again.

Carol said they should phone the police, but her husband said the police would think it was a wind-up, and who could blame them? The three of them then went upstairs, hoping to get a better look at the freakish caller from the safe vantage point of an upstairs window, but they could see nothing of the bizarre-looking woman. Eric suddenly remembered that he had not bolted the front and back doors and ran downstairs to do so.

The family talked about nothing else but the creepy little visitor for the remainder of that night. Eric, in particular, tried to explain her away, but found it impossible. They had all clearly seen bet not to mention Mr Jones. Andrew argued that the abnormally small old woman might have been some little child wearing a Halloween disguise, but his parents didn't even bother listening to his explanation, since it was nowhere near Halloween.

The three of them just sat in front of the gas fire; Carol lost in thought, as if she was reliving the spine-chilling encounter all over again, while her husband's eyes were darting from side to side, as if he was listening out for the old dwarf's return. They all finally retired to bed at 2am, but Andrew found sleep impossible and sat up in bed trying to read a comic called *2000 AD*, which featured the sci-fi character Judge Dredd. It was impossible to concentrate on the storyline of the comic because that surreal image of the little old lady kept replaying over and over in his mind. What was she? And why had she picked on their house? One thought in particular kept niggling away at his brain, no matter how he tried to suppress it. Could it be that there was a connection between her and the little figure he and Franno had seen at the Edge Lane house? With that uneasy thought still playing on his wears- mind, he finally fell into a shallow sleep.

Andrew had a strange dream during what was left of that night, in which ice-cold drops of water were falling on to his face, stinging his right cheek, and a raspy voice was saying, "Where is the brooch?"

"Where is my brooch?"

In the midst of this shadowy dream, Andrew suddenly had a vivid mental picture of the amethyst brooch, and awoke with a start. The little old woman was on his bed, kneeling on his chest, with her ghastly face pushed right up close to his. Her icy little index finger was rhythmically prodding his right cheek to emphasise each word as she repeatedly screeched out the same demand, "I said - where - is - that- brooch?" She was looking at him with such hatred and evil intent, it made his blood crawl.

Andrew knocked her off his chest with one mighty swipe from the back of his hand, and she landed on the carpet beneath his window with a faint thud. He leapt out of that bed, and out on to the landing. He looked back, not sure if he was dreaming. But no! He switched on the landing light, and there was the doll-sized woman peeping out at him from the doorway to his room. He ran straight into his parents' room and woke them up. His father told him to shut the door and keep it closed, and his son did just that by leaning against it. Carol got out of bed trembling, her eyes glued to the door, as Eric grabbed the confiscated air rifle from the wardrobe. He held the rifle stock in one hand and pulled the barrel downwards with the other. From a shelf in the wardrobe he took a steel ball-bearing from a round tin of point-22 ammunition and fed it into the rifle chamber, then snapped the barrel back into position. "Switch the light off," he said calmly.

Andrew did as he was asked and waited to see what his dad planned to do next. The landing light shone through the gap under the door, and that thin sliver of light was suddenly broken up by a black shadow, which kept moving slightly from side to side - the silhouette of the thing outside the door. The door was not a solid wooden one, but a hollow core door with foam blocks sandwiched between two thin boards. The end of the airgun barrel was placed against the door in a position calculated to send the ball-bearing right through it - and hopefully straight through the unearthly thing haunting the family on the other side.

There was a tremendous bang, which must have woken the whole neighbourhood, followed by a loud metal ring, presumably as the ball bearing ricocheted off the radiator on the landing wall opposite the bedroom door. The air rifle was reloaded, and then Eric dared to open the bedroom door, the smallest fraction, to survey the damage. The thing was standing there, looking up at him with a furious expression on its face, with its hands on its hips - and a neat round hole in the middle of its forehead! The door was quickly slammed in its face.

"The crazy thing's still there!" Eric whispered, leaning with his back on the door and wiping the beads of sweat from his face with the back of his hand. "I got it right in the head - but it's still just standing there. What does it want?" "Dad - I - er- I think I know what it wants," Andrew suddenly said, and he then confessed to his parents about the brooch he had taken from the house on Edge Lane, and the weird feeling he had had of being followed home.

"Why didn't you tell us all this earlier on?" his father asked, angrily.

"I didn't think -" was Andrew's honest reply. "Well, daft as it sounds, it looks like it's obviously got something to do with all this." And his father put his ear against the door and listened. Andrew meanwhile, peeped through the hole in the door made by the ball-bearing. He could see the diminutive old woman shuffling along the landing. "Mum, what do you think it is?" Andrew asked, looking worried sick.

"I haven't got a clue," his mother replied, breathless and hyperventillating. "- something to do with the devil, maybe - I don't know."

Carol was a very superstitious woman, and she kept hoping all this had been triggered by a nightmare. She looked to her husband for some kind of an answer, but he simply shook his head and said, "Listen! - It's on the stairs - I think it's leaving."

A few moments later Eric Johnson opened the door and found that the coast was clear. He cautiously stepped out on to the landing, still clutching the air rifle. He could hear bumps and hangings downstairs, as though someone was rifling through their drawers and cupboards. What was the miniature old woman up to? Keeping close together, Andrew and his father walked a little way along the passage.

"Oh, please come back," Carol pleaded. "You don't know what she's capable of. Andrew - stay in here."

But Andrew knew what he had to do. He tiptoed into his room and retrieved the brooch from the Doc Marten boot and handed it over to his father. "This is the brooch, Dad," he said, and placed it in his father's big rough palm.

"Right, let's hope it does the trick."

As soon as the brooch had changed hands, the thing could be heard dashing up the stairs.

Father and son scuttled back into the bedroom, and

just before they slammed the door, they saw the sinister little white figure come on to the landing, with a wild, wide-eyed look on its angry little face.

"Here!" Andrew's father threw the brooch at her, and she scurried towards it with an odd lopsided look of anticipation on her face. As soon as she had picked it up, her expression changed; her features relaxed and her crescent mouth turned slightly upwards into the beginnings of a smile. Having got what she had come for, she immediately turned and ran away, and her little boots could be heard jumping down the stairs.

After that night, the little old lady was thankfully never seen again at the Johnsons' Dovecot home.

So what exactly was the thing that followed Andrew home that night? When I mentioned this story on a radio programme many years ago, an old woman named Mrs Gallagher, who was once a member of a coven of witches from the Old Swan and Stoneycroft area, wrote to me and claimed that she was undoubtedly a 'fetch' - a shrunken, resurrected person - usually someone who had perpetrated many evil deeds while they were alive, and who was employed to carry out wicked tasks for a witch.

Mrs Gallagher went on to say that, in 1984, a brooch was stolen from a powerful witch named Clodagh - the so-called 'Witch of Edge Lane', about whom I have written in one of my earlier books. Mrs Gallagher intimated that the empty house on Edge Lane never appeared to be inhabited, because Clodagh actually lived in it, although she could not be seen by ordinary humans.

A man named John Crawford also got in touch with me to tell me how he had once attempted to move into the apparently vacant house, in 1981, but was unable to remain there because he would always find that someone, or something, had thrown his furniture around whenever he was out of the house. On one occasion his bed was tipped over in the middle of the night and he was thrown violently against the wall. He spoke to a previous occupant, who had experienced the same type of problem when he and his wife had tried to move into the house. This man said he had seen huge inexplicable shadows of spiders crawling on the ceiling, which had terrified his wife. After just a few days the family had decided that the place was uninhabitable and moved out.

Many people who lived near the house would also hear strange harp music playing at all hours of the night, and two women who passed by it on their way to the shops one wintry evening, were surprised to see a woman dressed in a dark blue gown, sitting toasting her toes in front of a blazing fire in a well-furnished room. Yet when the women passed by the house thirty minutes later, it looked empty again and its fireplace was all boarded up.

The alleged witch house is, at the time of writing, threatened with demolition, along with over four hundred other perfectly good houses on Edge Lane, which have had Government compulsory purchase orders slapped on them. The idea is to demolish these fine old houses to widen the road and so provide a 'gateway' into Liverpool. In reality, another piece of Liverpool's past is about to be destroyed by people who, for some inexplicable reason, seem hell-bent on erasing all the city's late-Georgian, Victorian and Edwardian architecture.

THE GEOMETRY OF DEATH

In the *Liverpool Mercury* in the late nineteenth century, a curious advertisement appeared for 'The Magic Shop', which opened for just a few days on 4 February 1880, at Number 112 Bold Street. I researched this advert for some time and discovered that a very dark tale lay behind it. This shop, as well as selling occult paraphernalia, trick novelties and conjuring apparatus, also sold books on real magic, and amongst them was one which bore a curious angular symbol, known as Lucifer's sigil.

The author of the book was a Victorian black magician known only as Aeslitend - old Saxon for 'law-breaker'. In 1858, Aeslitend was experimenting with a branch of occultism that involves geometry, and one of the experiments he carried out was to create a powerful spell to kill at a distance; its name is unknown, but we might well call it the 'Deltoid of Death'.

At midnight on Friday, 2 April 1858, Aeslitend recorded the sinister ritual in his book. He unfolded a map of Liverpool, and traced the geometric shape of a kite -known to mathematicians as a deltoid. At the four corners of the shape he drew four letters, including those of the so-called 'Lost English

Alphabet'. He then intoned a line from a dangerous grimoire (a magic text), and then probably sat back and waited for the results to come through via the newspapers. And he was not to be disappointed, for on each point of that map, on that very Saturday, four people hanged themselves.

On the Friday, Ellis Edwards, a forty-three-year-old man of Sumner Street, near Vauxhall Road, told his wife he was going to "finish himself before morning. It turned out to be no idle threat, for later that day he strung up a washing line around a hook on the ceiling of his parlour and hanged himself at 3am on Saturday morning.

The second suicide of that fateful Saturday took place at around 4am on Northampton Street, off Leeds Street. John Hand, a thirty-five-year-old cart-owner and fruiterer, was found hanging from his bedpost by two knotted handkerchiefs. Drink was blamed in this case, but those who knew John said he was not a man to entertain suicidal thoughts, even when inebriated.

The third 'coincidental suicide', as the police chose to call it, occurred later that day when fifty-six-year-old Jane Prophet, of Number 7 Alfred Street, Wavertree, hanged herself with her apron string at 7pm. She had not even been depressed, let alone showing any signs of feeling suicidal in the time leading up to her tragic death, so when her friend Mrs Keefe found her at 9pm, she was deeply shocked.

The fourth self-hanging took place only about ten minutes after the previous one, at an empty, derelict house on Fountains Road, Walton. A vagrant, who was never identified, had hanged himself from what was left of the banister, and was found to have a full bottle of rum in his pocket. Once again drink was blamed as the principal cause of the suicide.

The police of the day failed to take a map view of these four incidents, but had they taken the trouble to mark them up in that way, they would have seen how the suicide sites formed a perfect deltoid shape. Thirty years later, the police would be equally ignorant of the perfect rhombus shape that Jack the Ripper would carve on to the map of London's East End with his first four murders.

There are some who maintain that Zodiac, a serial killer who operated mainly around northern California in the 1960s, also planned his murders geographically, to form occult symbols. Zodiac was never caught, and delighted in taunting the police with messages and clues in various complex ciphers.

In Aeslitend's little black book he had marked out sites on a map that looks suspiciously like the rural Liverpool of the 1850s, and one of these marked locations seems to be Bloody Acre, a mysterious tract of accursed land lying next to Childwall Church, which has been the scene of many dark and paranormal goings on for many years.

In 1969, George, one of my readers, who lived close to the enigmatic site, told me how once he had been watching a fine white horse grazing on Bloody Acre one lovely summer afternoon, when all of a sudden a huge shadow materialised on the land. The horse whinnied in alarm and then reared up on its hind legs. It galloped off, leaping over a stone wall into Score Lane.

George then watched, open-mouthed, as an

amorphous dark looming mass, seemingly made of some type of black vapour, made a slow descent into the middle of Bloody Acre. Seconds later, the eerie phenomenon ceased, and the sun shone over the field again, as if someone had turned on a switch. Today, Bloody Acre is an important wildlife reserve, which is just as well, since there is a chilling legend that maintains that a terrible curse of death shall be upon anyone who tries to build upon that field.

One of the other sites marked in Aeslitend's book seems to be a location now covered by Spinney Woods in Kirkby. The woods were once part of Lord Sefton's estate, and formed part of his hunting grounds. Spinney Woods, like Bloody Acre, also has something of a supernatural reputation.

In the late 1970s, two girls were picking blackberries in the woods when they noticed a pair of boots sticking out of the brambles. When they parted the brambles they came across the body of a man, lying dead in the undergrowth. The two girls ran off to inform the police, but a thorough search of the woods revealed no body. It transpired that this dead man's apparition had apparently been seen several times before and was believed to be the ghost of a murderer who, in 1964, committed suicide in the wood, after battering a young housewife to death inside her Croxteth home.

THE WIND FROM HELL

The longer revenge is delayed, the crueller and bloodier it will eventually become, both in this world and in the world of the supernatural. Where blood has been unjustly spilt, the tree of forgetfulness can never flourish, and this is the grim theme of both this and the following story - supernatural vengeance and retribution from beyond the grave.

In the autumn of 1838, John Hunt, a well-to-do middle-aged cotton-merchant of Ashton-under-Lyne, residing at Canning Street, became engaged to twenty-seven-year-old music teacher Anne Jones, who lived in the Toxteth Park area of the city. Hunt seems to have had something of a chequered past, but he covered it up to some extent by occasionally embroidering a false history of his life.

One day a man named Scott recognised Hunt as he and Anne stood near the Old Infirmary amongst the crowds watching the foundation stone of St George's Hall being laid; an event simultaneous with the coronation ceremony of Queen Victoria. When Scott accosted him, Hunt swore he had never set eyes on him in his life, and when he accused Hunt of committing an outrage against a serving-maid at the Old King's Head public house in Chester, the devious businessman stormed off in a rage, dragging a bemused Anne behind him.

Anne was a highly naive and gullible young woman and seemed to be totally blind to the inconsistencies in John's account of his past life, despite the fact that she had been betrayed once before, by her previous fiancé. She did not even suspect him of having not one, but two, affairs behind her back.

During Christmas 1837, Anne received an anonymous letter claiming that John Hunt had, since the summer, been having an affair with a poverty-stricken gypsy girl of sixteen named Maggie. The girl scraped a living by selling bunches of lavender, heather and shamrock, as well as peg-dolls - anything to survive. At first, she succumbed to his charms and fell madly in love with John, but her Romany intuition soon warned her that he had a dark, unfaithful side. They say love can be blind sometimes, and Maggie made the fatal mistake of initially doubting her grave suspicions about her lover, for she desperately wanted to stay with him. She chose not to believe the letter's contents and threw the anonymous warning on the fire, for she also wanted to remain his wife-to-be.

Then one day Maggie was on Duke Street, selling her little wares, when she was shocked and then utterly heartbroken to see John Hunt walking along with Anne Jones on his arm. The music teacher was splendidly attired in a dress of dark blue brocaded velvet, old point and black satin, and she looked so impossibly beautiful that Maggie felt completely crushed. How could a simple girl like herself ever hope to compete with such elegance, wealth and refinement? As the couple passed her by, the poor girl burst into tears and bowed her head, and Anne, a sympathetic soul, rushed over to ask the gypsy what was troubling her. John instantly realised what had happened and quickly dragged Anne across Duke Street and on to his house, lest his treachery be disclosed by a mere chit of a girl.

Anne naturally thought her fiancé's behaviour was strange and for the first time she began to question his character. She then recalled the claims of that anonymous letter she had received - about John's alleged affair with a gypsy girl. Her head was spinning in turmoil and she wanted with all her heart to deny her suspicions. But she knew that hearts were unreliable in these matters and she had to find out what sort of a man she was intending to marry. She resolved to go and seek out the young Romany in the morning, so she could quiz her about the supposed infidelity.

That night, a drunken John Hunt caught up with Maggie as she stood outside a public house in the town, still selling her wares, though the hour was late. She had not eaten since that morning and was visibly drooping, but the cad grabbed her by the arm and dragged her to a secluded alley at the rear of the pub. There, amongst the rubbish and filth, he warned her that he would slit her throat if she so much as breathed a word to Anne about the affair they had had. To cut down the likelihood of her disobeying his orders, he insisted that, from now on, she should ply her trade up in the north end of the town, near to her lodging house.

Now in no doubt that her worst suspicions about John Hunt had been confirmed, Maggie felt nothing but loathing for him. As a woman scorned, she looked him straight in the eye said, "I curse you, John Hunt; I curse you and your coming marriage - and your business!" and with that, the young gypsy maiden ran off into the moonless night.

Not long afterwards, on 6 January 1839, John Hunt took Anne to a ball at the house of a fellow cotton merchant on Hope Street, and then, at around midnight, full of whisky and false affection, he walked her home in the moonlight. They were strolling through the delph of St James's Cemetery, hand in hand, when Anne suddenly stopped dead in her tracks and turned to him. With unaccustomed boldness, she asked him directly, "Have you been true to me, John, as I have been true to you since we first met?"

"Why, yes, of course, my darling, I have been true constantly!"

To emphasise his point, John released her hand and stepped back with a look of mock horror on his face.

"Then swear upon it, John Hunt!"

Anne now had tears ready to fall from her large sorrowful eyes; eyes which no longer had any innocence left in them.

"Anne, my darling, why do you cry? Has someone -" John reached out to her.

She shrank back from him, "Swear upon it that you have been faithful to me!"

At the top of his drunken voice John bellowed out

across the place of the dead, "I have never been untrue to you, Anne! May the earth open up and swallow me if I am lying!"

Anne sobbed into her handkerchief, for from the tone of his voice and his lack of respect for this place of the dead, she sensed he was not telling the truth. She saw it clearly now, he was just like the last man she had loved and lost two years ago. How could she have been so naive as to allow the same thing to happen again? John Hunt's drunken features contorted into an insincere smile, and then he roared out, with his head craned back and his eyes fixed on the moon, "May the dead rise from their graves if I have ever been unfaithful to my sweetest, darlingest fiancée - spinster of the parish - the ever lovely, Anne Jones!

What took place next would go down in the annals of Liverpool's supernatural history. As Anne was still digesting this last sarcastic outburst, a hurricane-force wind gusted up from nowhere in the cemetery, simultaneously whipping off John Hunt's hat and Anne Jones's bonnet, to be lost amongst the crumbling gravestones. The mighty wind flung Anne clear across the graveyard, and then in a howling, whistling fury, it ripped up trees that had entangled their roots around rotten, water-logged coffins, and in the act of wrenching up these oaken sentinels of the cemetery, corpses and their splintering boxes were hurled into the night air.

The worm-infested body of a quite recent cholera victim, in a state of advancing decomposition, landed on John Hunt torso-first, and its skeletal arms swung around him upon impact, encircling him in a grotesque embrace. Ghastly syrupy brown-red blood spattered all over him, and the soft buttery adipose fat and loose jelly bowels of its lower abdomen stuck to his hands, as he wrestled in a frenzy to extricate himself from the corpse.

Throughout all this Anne was screaming in terror, but her cries were swamped by the roaring devil-gales. She was forced to watch as a massive granite slab was tossed into the air by the thick gnarled root of a felled oak and came hurtling back down towards John Hunt. The philanderer desperately tried to dive out of the way, but the flying gravestone grazed his shoulder and spun him round like a child's spinning top.

Under the ancient wan eye of the moon, more trees were toppled and their roots unearthed the dead on this most terrible Judgement Night. This was not the glorious resurrection promised by most world religions, but a cruel and vicious war of the wind, waged by the elements. The remains of the dearly departed, as well as the not-missed-at-all, were thrown alike into the air, catapulted by the uprooting of the trees, which the wind still knocked down like skittles. Skulls, bones, tattered burial shrouds, embalmed men, women, infants and children of all walks of life rained down upon John Hunt, in what must surely be one of the most terrible acts of vengeance ever conceived.

Anne struggled to her feet and somehow made it out of the cemetery, unable to breathe properly, because the whirlwind was sucking the oxygen from her lungs. John Hunt was blinded in one eye by tempest-driven splinters when a tree smashed against a looming marble headstone. He staggered along after Anne with a dozen skulls rolling after him, but in the noise and confusion he fell headfirst into an open grave, spraining his wrist as he landed amongst the sludge and bones. It was then that he remembered his blasphemous challenge to God - to let the earth open up and swallow him if he had been untrue to Anne. He whimpered pathetically for forgiveness now, but by the time he had climbed out of the grave, his fiancée was nowhere to be seen.

As Hunt leaned into the demonic gale on Hope Street, and tried to make his way home, blade-sharp slates rained down all around him. A passing cart, abandoned by its terrified driver, was overturned, and its horse fell down on its side. The stricken animal's legs kicked futilely in the air; its nostrils flared and the whites of its eyes were like two great saucers, but like a beetle on its back, it could not right itself and the wicked killer wind blasted on down Hope Street, cruelly dragging the unfortunate shrieking horse across the cobbles, flaying its skin to the bone in places.

Entire rooftops were blown clean off by the windstorm, and many died in the freak weather on the so-called "Night of the Big Wind", which would be remembered with dread by the townspeople for many decades to come. The destructive hurricane continued on unabated throughout the night and it did not burn itself out until the following afternoon. Houses were demolished, ships were sunk, and many people lost their lives, crushed to death as they slept in their beds by falling chimney stacks.

A traumatised John Hunt was left with only one eye, and without his beautiful fiancée, for the first thing Anne did after that apocalyptic night of the hell wind, was to break off their engagement. If ever there was an omen bringing an unequivocal message, this had to be it. Hunt also lost his cotton business, again as a direct result of that hurricane. He held many shares in stock at the North-Shore Mill, which was an important cotton factory situated on the west bank of the Leeds and Liverpool Canal, but the wind blew in every single pane of glass in the building. The high-velocity Aeolian currents then ripped off the roof, like the lid off a sardine can, and then destroyed the machinery and scattered and shredded over a thousand valuable bales of cotton across the north-end of the city.

A furious blizzard of this shredded cotton snow fell to earth over many square miles of north Liverpool, including the ruins of Kirkdale Gaol, which had sustained heavy structural damage, including a main wall that was demolished by the gales. Hunt had not been adequately insured for a loss of such magnitude and he lost everything he owned in those few short hours.

Hundreds died that night and the destruction to property was unprecedented. One of the people who survived was Maggie, the teenaged gypsy girl. She later met and married a decent young man, who unlike Hunt, proved to be faithful and loving and she went to live with him in Chester. One of the last sights she beheld before she left Liverpool for good, was John Hunt - not the wealthy cotton merchant she had once known, but a man reduced to penury, walking the streets in filthy shabby clothes, begging for money. Maggie must have been satisfied that her curse had worked to perfection on its intended target, though unfortunately it had also wreaked so much havoc, death and destruction on the innocent throughout the whole city.

THE NIGHT MARE

Animals have souls, no matter what certain religious groups might claim, and I have collected many accounts of creatures great and small being seen, felt and heard, after their physical deaths.

In 2004, a woman named Barbara, who lived on West Derby's Leyfield Road, woke up at three o'clock one morning to the distinctive sound of a bird flapping about in her bedroom, which was pitch-black at that time. The fluttering and chirping sounded exactly like her beloved budgerigar George, when he was allowed out of his cage, but Barbara knew he was asleep in that cage in the living room downstairs.

At 6.30am, Barbara got up and went downstairs to make her customary early morning cup of tea. Her next job was always to go into the living room to remove the cover off George's cage, but on this morning she found the little bird lying dead on the bottom of its cage. Barbara was naturally very upset by the loss of her little feathered friend, but it was only later that day that she recalled the sound of the bird flying about in her bedroom in the early hours, and wondered if it could have been George saying his last goodbyes before passing on into the spirit world.

A similar unexplained incident happened many years

ago at the Aigburth home of a certain doctor. The doctor's cat Tibbs had just died, aged eighteen - not a bad innings in terms of feline years. The doctor and his family discussed what to do about another pet and decided to buy a new kitten immediately, in the hope of trying to alleviate the loss of their old pet, although no cat could ever replace Tibbs.

On the evening of the day after Tibbs had passed away, the new kitten, Dandy, was finding its feet in its new home, when it was approached by a very familiar moggy. The doctor and his wife gasped in amazement, because there was Tibbs. The old cat padded into the lounge from the direction of the hall, just as it had always done. It sniffed at Dandy, meowed at the doctor's wife, as if showing its approval of their new acquisition, then turned and walked back into the hall. The doctor went after Tibbs, even though he had buried him at the bottom of the garden that very morning, but he found the hallway empty. Nevertheless, the cat was seen several more times over the years by family members and their friends, and on one occasion, the doctor even felt the purring cat sleeping curled up next to his feet on the end of his bed, just as Tibbs had often used to do.

In the early 1860s, a Colonel Charles MacIver, managing partner of the Cunard Line of steamships, was throwing a grand party at his imposing residence, Dovecot House, which was built in 1829 by a John Tarbock. The manor house stood on land that is occupied today by Dovecot Park, close to the junction of Pilch Lane and Dovecot Avenue.

During the party at Dovecot House, MacIver boasted of his top notch equestrian skills, and a guest named Ralph Walsh, sick of hearing MacIver sing his own praises, challenged him to a midnight gallop around the estate. MacIver accepted the challenge with gusto, even though it was expressly against his wife's wishes, and so, at precisely midnight, Walsh set off on his horse Dobby, and MacIver tore off after him on his black filly, Shadow.

Both riders raced in a great circle of a half-mile radius, across fields, through a pond, over hedges and fences. MacIver arrived at the agreed finishing point first, to a great cheer from the late-night revellers. Almost a minute passed before Walsh limped in on his exhausted horse, which almost collapsed under the strain its rider had put it through. MacIver tried to shake hands with Walsh but the latter refused and instead demanded water for his exhausted horse, after which he took himself off home.

The next day, MacIver's exquisite thoroughbred mare was found dead in its stable. An autopsy on her established that she had been poisoned with a certain wild fern which is fatal to horses, even when ingested in very small quantities. Ralph Walsh was immediately suspected of being the malicious poisoner, still reeling as he was from his humiliation of the previous night. But there were no witnesses, so nothing could be proved.

A year later, Walsh fell on hard times after a business venture went disastrously wrong, and swallowing his pride, he called on MacIver one stormy night, pleading that he had no other place to stay. The bailiffs had emptied his home of every last stick of furniture and every last pot and pan and he had been sleeping on the floorboards of his house ever since, without even a lump of coal to burn in the grate. He had been forced to go into the woods to forage for wood in order to keep warm.

MacIver was in two minds as to whether he should allow the destitute fellow into his home and he mentioned the poisoning of his beloved horse. "If I had an ounce of sense, sir, I would have you thrashed and thrown off the premises. How dare you come here begging for mercy, after such a low and dastardly trick?" Ralph Walsh responded to this denunciation by asking for a Bible to be brought to him that instant, so he could swear his innocence. Mrs MacIver ran and fetched the family Bible, and Walsh placed his hand upon it and solemnly declared, "Before Almighty God, I swear I did not kill the horse, Shadow."

MacIver, probably naively, took this to be positive proof that Walsh was telling the truth. Their friendship restored, at least on the surface, that night the bankrupt was treated to a hearty supper and given a bed in one of the many sumptuous spare rooms in the manor house. However, during the night Walsh fell ill and a doctor had to be summoned. The physician diagnosed a high fever and advised MacIver to keep his guest confined to bed for at least a week, or until the fever had subsided. MacIver felt he had no choice. He could not turf a sick man out on to the streets and so reluctantly he gave the servants instructions to care for Walsh until he had recovered.

On the second night something terrifying and inexplicable took place. It was exactly one year since the shocking poisoning of Shadow, and at midnight, the sound of galloping hooves was heard, first way off in the distance, and then in the grounds of Dovecot

House.

A delirious Ralph Walsh tossed about on his sweat-soaked pillows with a look of pure horror on his face. He asked a servant who had brought him his medicine who it was that was riding around the house at such a late hour, but the servant saw and heard nothing when he glanced out the window. Walsh asked for the bedside oil lamp to be turned up to admit a little more illumination, as the uncanny sounds of the dead horse pricked at his conscience and unsettled his fevered mind.

A heavy shower of hail clattered deafeningly against the windows of Dovecot House, and Charles MacIver watched the dramatic hailstorm and flashes of lightning as he smoked a pipe under the covered portico at the entrance to his grandiose dwelling. As he leaned on one of the pillars supporting the portico, he saw something that defied all reason. A sleek black mare was galloping like the wind across the fields facing the house, and was coming directly towards him. As the horse thundered nearer through the hailstorm, MacIver opened his mouth in total disbelief. He quickly recognised that horse. How could he not? For it was none other than his beloved Shadow.

Wind as sharp as a razor slammed into MacIver, knocking him sideways from the pillar. The icy blast forced open the front doors of the manor house, and a heartbeat later, the ghostly black filly approached at high speed with her horseshoes sparking like firecrackers on the gravel drive. She leapt up the five steps of the portico in one great bound, then galloped straight through the front doorway and into the great entrance hall. MacIver ran inside after the horse and watched as she charged towards the elegantly carpeted sweeping staircase. With flecks of foam falling from her mouth and covering her sweating heaving flanks. the mare bolted up the whole flight of stairs and then dashed along the landing - straight towards the room where Walsh lay battling the mystery fever.

Ralph Walsh and the servant who was attending him could not help but hear the unearthly cacophony of heavy thuds outside the door, and the servant opened it to find out what was happening. The ghostly horse barged through the doorway in a flash, passing straight through the startled servant, who felt an ice-cold chill course through his veins-as it did so. He collapsed to the floor, weak as a kitten from shock, and than saw Charles MacIver rush into the bedroom seconds later. The master of Dovecot House and his servant watched the ghostly mare rear up on her great hind legs over Walsh's sickbed. The mare seemed to fill the entire room and Walsh was screaming for mercy, and hiding his face under the blankets. The horse brought down her front hooves on Walsh's body several times - yet inflicted no actual physical harm - but the fevered man suddenly clutched at his throat with both hands.

The long windows burst open and the wind tore the blankets off the bed and extinguished the oil lamp, plunging the room into total darkness. Walsh emitted one last ghastly-sounding scream, then sank back silent on to the pillows. The mare raised her great head, flattening her ears and baring her teeth as she whinnied in triumph. Her deadly mission accomplished, she galloped towards the open window and vaulted through it, like some latter day Pegasus, out into the night.

MacIver and the servant had watched all this in stunned disbelief, but they ran to the window and looked out, expecting to see the phantom horse in the grounds down below, but it had already vanished. The hailstorm stopped abruptly seconds later and the room became suffused with a deathly aura. The servant rummaged round in the darkness and finally located the oil lamp. When it was lit both he and MacIver immediately looked over to the bed, where Walsh lay dead. His body seemed to have shrunk with death and could barely be discerned beneath the bedclothes, and still written on its face was a look of extreme terror. It was later established that Walsh had died from heart failure, no doubt brought on by the ghostly equine visitation.

Until Dovecot House was demolished in 1928, a ghostly horse was often seen galloping through its grounds in the dead of night, and this same long-dead horse was also heard entering the house, its iron hooves clattering through the great hallway, and up the staircase, seeking its prey. Shadow is still seeking vengeance from her poisoner and still haunts Dovecot Park, even to this day.

BACK FROM THE WAR

Not all ghosts haunt the place of their death and they can be encountered in locations thousands of miles away from the site where their lives ended. Take, for example, the case of twenty-two-year-old World War One airman Eldred Bowyer-Bower, who died after being shot down over France, near St Leger, early in the morning of 19 March 1917.

Around the time of this brave young man's death, his half-sister, Dorothy Spearman, was staying at a hotel in Calcutta, where she was sitting quietly sewing and talking to her baby, when she was suddenly overcome by a strong urge to turn around. She did so, and was pleasantly surprised, if not more than a little shocked, to see her half-brother Eldred standing watching her, with a mischievous smile on his face.

"Why, Eldred, fancy coming out here to see me!" cried Dorothy in delight. "What a delightful surprise."

She had thought Eldred was still fighting thousands

of miles away in France, and she asked him to wait a minute while she put the baby down in a safer place, so she could greet him properly. She quickly tucked the baby up in its cot and then turned round, arms outstretched, ready to give Eldred a welcoming kiss and a hug, only to find that he was no longer anywhere to be seen. She thought he was playing some kind of trick on her, by hiding somewhere, but there were few places to hide in the hotel bedroom and though she looked inside and behind the wardrobe, behind the curtains and under the bed, she failed to find him. She suddenly became intensely worried, and felt dizzy and sick with concern for his safety, experiencing an overwhelming feeling that a terrible disaster had befallen Eldred.

Her worst fears were confirmed when, two weeks later, Dorothy Spearman learned of her half-brother's disappearance over France and eventually received the unbearable news that he had been killed, along with the date of his death. She immediately realised that Eldred had visited her from beyond the grave on the morning of his death, and she was not the only relative to receive such a visit on that fateful morning. The dead airman's young niece had also seen him and ran up to her mother's bedroom to tell her that her uncle was downstairs. The child's mother said that could not possibly be the case, because he was fighting in France, but the little girl was most insistent that she had seen him.

On that same morning - 19 March 1917 - Mrs Watson, a close friend of the airman's family, wrote to Eldred's mother, saying she had just received a strong impression of her son, which had made her fear for his safety.

This 'haunting from a distance' is a widespread phenomenon in the world of the occult, and in the next chapter I will look at several similar long-distance ghosts which are at large in Liverpool.

LONG-DISTANCE BEATLE GHOSTS

Locally, there are many 'long-distance ghosts' that haunt Liverpool. At Gambier Terrace, Hope Street, and nearby Percy Street, the ghost of a pallid-faced man with a swept-back quiff and sunglasses is thought to be that of artist and musician, Stuart Sutcliffe, who lodged with his best friend (and fellow Art School student) John Lennon in the early 1960s, before the Beatles hit the big time. The other phantom which is often seen accompanying the apparition, is that of a sharp-suited man in a red or orange turban and a heavy, long black moustache. His identity is unknown. Sutcliffe also had a flat at Number 9 Percy Street at one point, and the ghost which bears a striking resemblance to him has been seen in that street as well for many years.

Around 9.50pm on Monday, 26 May 2008 - the Spring Bank Holiday - a woman called Lisa was out walking her Jack Russell from her home off Hope Street towards Upper Parliament Street, and as she passed the southern entrance of Gambier Terrace, she came upon a youth dressed in a black polo neck sweater and dark suit, standing by bushes. He wore shades and had his head slightly bowed. Another man stood about six feet away from him, looking towards a window in the flat. He had a black walrus moustache, wore a dark red turban, a dark blue tie, white shirt and dark grey suit. Something about the static figures struck an odd note. Neither of the men looked at Lisa, or seemed aware of her presence, but her dog started to howl, and then barked at the strangers. Embarrassed, Lisa pulled the Jack Russell away from them, and tried to get her to be quiet, and when she looked back a few seconds later, the two men had gone. They had literally vanished into thin air. Lisa was so spooked by the experience she avoided taking her dog through that area again after that nightfall.

This report does not stand in isolation; many other people have written to me over the years to tell me about Sutcliffe's ghost. Sutcliffe lies buried in the graveyard of St Michael's Church, in Huyton. I once mentioned the alleged spectre to Beatles historian, Spencer Leigh, and he was very sceptical about the sightings, because, as he rightly pointed out, Sutcliffe actually died in Hamburg, on 10 April 1962, so he questioned why his ghost would haunt his former residences in Liverpool, some five hundred and thirty miles away from the place of his death. Yet such a phenomenon is actually rather more common in the world of the supernatural than you might expect.

John Lennon was murdered in New York, in 1980, but there have been quite a few sightings of his ghost three thousand three hundred miles away from the Big Apple, right here in his hometown. It is alleged that the Beatles once made a pact with each other, that whoever died first was to send a message back from the after-life to the three surviving Beatles. In 1995, during the Beatles recording of *Free As a Bird*,

McCartney was reported as saying he felt as if John was actually there, perhaps in spirit. There were also alleged spirit audio messages from John, which appeared in the final mix of the record, and the words 'Made for John Lennon' can be heard at the end of the *Free As a Bird* track - and when this message is played backwards, it becomes the George Formbyesque quip: 'Turned out nice again'.

In the year 2000, Mr Carney, an elderly motorist from Crosby, was driving down Church Road South in Wavertree with his forty-year-old daughter Christine in the passenger, seat, when he lost control of his vehicle and smashed into an oncoming car. Mr Carney, his daughter, and the woman in the other car were all wearing seat belts, and the injuries they suffered were thankfully minimal. However, Christine suffered shock from the impact, and got out of the car in a daze after the crash and walked to the pavement on the corner of Newcastle Road. A man with long brown shoulder length hair and wire-rimmed glasses was standing there with his arms outstretched. He wore a white suit. Chrissy thought he was someone she knew because he looked so familiar, and the man even embraced her and although she cannot now remember exactly what he said, they were reassuring words. After she had calmed down somewhat, he gently coaxed her to go back to her father, who was still sitting in the car, to see if he was alright, which she did. Chrissy halted a moment to glance back at the man in the white suit and saw that he was no longer there. It was then that it suddenly came to her who he was - John Lennon - a man who had been dead for twenty years.

Chrissy was not even a Beatles fan and could not

understand why she had 'hallucinated' John Lennon, of all people. What she did not know was that Lennon's white-suited ghost had been encountered many times on Newcastle Road - where the Beatle had once lived (at Number 9) during part of his childhood. The same ghost has allegedly also been seen at Strawberry Fields, which was once a Salvation Army Children's Home on Beaconsfield Road, and where Lennon the boy played with the orphans and attended garden parties and fetes.

The earliest reports I have of Lennon's ghost being seen in Liverpool are in June 1990, and the sightings peak that month, on the very evening of Sir Paul McCartney's 'Let it Be' concert at the King's Dock. What was thought to be a Lennon lookalike from the Abbey Road era was seen outside of the church of St Nicholas by a group of people, and all of them said the figure gave the characteristic peace sign before it vanished in front of their eyes. These reports came in from a wide range of witnesses, ranging from tourists, cabbies, passersby and even a policeman.

Note: One evening in August 2010, whilst walking down Beaconsfield Road, I and a person who does not want to be named saw about six or seven ghosts of boys of about 8 to 10 years old, gazing at us through the gates of Strawberry Field. When I attempted to approach them, they vanished one by one, and the person I was with ran off in such a state of fear, he was almost knocked down by a car. All of the ghosts were dressed in old fashioned coats, and a few wore dark shorts that went to their knees. Many of them had short haircuts, and the one who seemed most prominent had a sandy coloured basin haircut. I am convinced these are the ghosts of orphans who attended the orphanage at Strawberry Field, and I strongly feel that Lennon's ghost associates with these earthbound phantoms.

BLACK SPIDER

In 1997, I received a letter from Betty, who used to live on Pulford Avenue, in Prenton, in the 1960s. In it Betty told me how, as a twelve-year-old girl, she got into bed as normal one night in August 1967, at around 10.30pm. She read her favourite girls' comic for a while, then switched off the light and was soon fast sleep. Some time later, Betty felt something cold land on her right eyelid, and she opened her eyes to find some kind of creepy-crawly probing about in the folds of her eyelid. Instinctively she tried to reach up and flick it off, but found she could not move. She tried to scream, because she had a severe phobia of spiders, but to her horror, she found she was not able to utter even the tiniest sound. She could just make out the silhouette of a man standing at the foot of her bed, laughing at her. The spider-like creature nipped painfully at the girl's eyelid and suddenly she recovered the power of movement. She brushed the insect from her eye and felt its cold hard body plop on to her left wrist. She then ran screaming past the shadowy stranger on her way to the bedroom door. Once out, she almost fell down the stairs in her rush to get away from the horrors in her bedroom, and ran straight into the living room, where her father, a keen amateur astronomer, was in the middle of watching *The Sky at Night* programme on the television. He was furious when Betty barged in screaming about some sort of spider; this phobia of hers was getting beyond a joke. Then she told him that there was a man in her room, and his attitude changed immediately. He rushed straight upstairs, but found her bedroom completely empty - no spiders, and certainly no creepy strangers.

The commotion awakened Betty's mother, who had been sleeping soundly in bed and her husband said Betty-had just had a nightmare about a spider and 'the bogeyman'. What else was he to think?

On the following morning, Betty's mother was visited by her friend Connie, who lived around the corner, on Waterpark Road. The two women sat down in the kitchen to have a good old natter over a pot of tea. Then Connie happened to mention something that sent a shiver down Betty's mother's spine. She said that her eleven-year-old daughter Alice had wet the bed after suffering a terribly vivid nightmare of a man dressed all in black who had put a spider on her eye, and when she woke up she felt the spider crawling all over her eyelid but was unable to move to dislodge it. She had suffered a fit as a result and the doctor had to be called out and prescribed her tranquillisers.

Connie assumed her daughter had dreamt up the spider, until she came across an unusually large black spider, of a type she had never seen before, under her pillow when she came to make her bed.

"When did all this happen, Connie?" Betty's mother inquired, intrigued by the similarity of the story to her own daughter's experience.

"Mm, let me see - I think it was about half-past eleven," Connie replied.

That was exactly when Betty had come screaming

into the living room the night before. Betty's mother had not mentioned this incident to Connie or anyone else. Well, that was in 1967, and I suppose, at a push, you could put the two 'nightmares' (if that is what they were) down to coincidence, but then I received an email, in 2002, from a man named Doug Scott. In 1971, when Doug was fifteen, and living in a tenement block in south Liverpool, he went to bed one night at around 11pm and woke up at around four in the morning, unable to move. There was a strange glimmering orange light on the ceiling, as if there were a fire outside his bedroom window and it was shining into his room. All of a sudden, a silhouetted figure of a man bent over him and in a creepy low voice, the stranger said, "Hello, Doug!" Doug then felt something cold crawl haltingly across his right cheek, as if it were exploring new territory. From the way it felt, he was sure it was a large spider. The teenager had a terrible fear of arachnids and he could feel his heart pounding with the stress of it. Then the spider crawled over Doug's right eye, obscuring his vision in that eye. The boy was so traumatised he defecated and then suddenly found he was able to cry out again. He jumped up and wiped the spider from his eye and ran out of the room in fear of his life. The figure was still standing by his bed as he fled from the room, and the peculiar pattern of shimmering light was still illuminating the bedroom ceiling.

When Doug returned to the bedroom with his father and uncle, the room was in darkness and there was no shadowy man or orange light shining on the ceiling. Every night for that whole week, Doug had to suffer the torture of that repulsive arachnid crawling over his face and sometimes also his hand, but try as he might, he was always unable to capture or kill the eight-legged menace.

In 2006 I received a letter from a Mrs Marsden, which contained a tale that is remarkably similar to Doug Scott's. In 1988, when she was thirty-six, she went to stay with a relative who had just lost her husband to help her with all the funeral arrangements. This relative lived on Richard Kelly Drive, which runs from Townsend Lane in Anfield, to Walton Hall Avenue, in Walton.

At around 11.30pm on the eve of the funeral, Mrs Marsden went upstairs to sleep in the spare room. She had only been asleep for about fifteen minutes when she suddenly awoke, and discovered that she could not move an inch. She couldn't even blink, or move her mouth. At first, she was only aware of voices coming from the television set in the lounge downstairs. Then suddenly she saw the shadow of a figure projected on to the ceiling, and prayed that it was that of her relative, coming into the room to help her. But it belonged to a complete stranger, in the form of a black silhouette without any discernible features - until he leaned over her and looked deep into her eyes.

His skin was bloodless and so white it was almost blue, and in contrast, his eyes were coal black, with no whites to them at all - just an unnatural blackness. He mouth slowly fell open and out plopped a large black insect of some sort. It landed on Mrs Marsden's eyeball. She was so repelled by this that she passed out. When she came to she got up and turned on the light and there, scuttling across the floor, was a large black spider with a thick hairy body and bent spindly legs.

She grabbed a heavy book and dropped it on the spider and then ran downstairs. She returned minutes later with her relative, who carefully lifted the edge of the book - but the spider was nowhere to be seen.

Mrs Marsden was unable to settle down in that room again and so she went downstairs to sleep on the sofa. She was still feeling very jittery, and decided she would sleep with the lamp on. As soon as she had closed her eyes and was starting to relax by trying to put all thoughts of the creepy stranger and the spider from her mind, she heard a faint pattering sound which startled her and set her nerves jangling anew. She opened her eyes, and there, crawling along the wall towards her was an identical black spider to the one she had seen up in the spare bedroom.

She reflexively picked up the nearest thing, which happened to be a small scatter cushion, and whacked the spider with it. The eight-legged stalker dropped like a stone, landing behind the sofa, and Mrs Marsden quickly got up and switched on the main lights. Fearful of what she might find, she looked behind the sofa, but could see no sign of the spider, dead or alive. She stayed up all that night drinking one cup of coffee after another to keep her alert should the spider make a reappearance, and was in an exhausted state by the time she attended the funeral later that morning. Despite feeling sorry for her bereaved relative, she never dared set foot in that house on Richard Kelly Drive again.

A LOVELY OLD LAMP

In 2005 there was an intriguing case reported to me about a ghost that flitted around to three different houses spaced miles apart. The story began in January 2005, when two robbers noticed a light in a window one night in a house off Green Lane, Old Swan. One of the thieves had recently moved into a flat opposite this old house and he had cased the property with the aid of powerful binoculars. The thief, whose name was Peter, had established that there was no one in the front parlour of the house and no furniture, so he was disappointed. The only light in the empty room came from a tall floor-lamp, with a stand about five-and-a-half feet in height.

Peter was not your average thief and housebreaker; he was also something of an antiques expert, and slowly turning the thumb-wheel of the binoculars to bring the image of the lamp into crystal-sharp focus, he saw that it seemed to be a 1912 Bigelow and Kennard floor-lamp. It would have been worth around fifteen-hundred quid all day long, if some Philistine had not modified it with a modern light-bulb socket and switch.

Nevertheless, Peter decided it was still worth taking.

He noticed how the lamp came on at 8pm each evening, and he did a further bit of reconnoitring. He walked casually past the parlour window and saw the lamp was plugged into an old voltage time-switch. Peter watched the parlour for three days, then, satisfied that the house was uninhabited, he made his move. He broke in using a home-made skeleton key at three o'clock one morning and dismantled the lamp in the back parlour. As he was leaving via the backyard, it suddenly struck him as odd that the electricity had been left switched on in an empty house.

Peter's girlfriend Lindsay took a liking to the antique lamp, and she took it home to her flat on Rathbone Road, where it was placed in the corner behind her leather sofa. A few days later, just before lunchtime, when Lindsay was out at her place of work (at a certain shop in the city centre) she received a call on her mobile phone from her friend Susannah, who said she had seen two women, dressed in black old-fashioned clothes, sitting on Lindsay's sofa. After calling at Lindsay's ground-floor flat and getting no answer, Susannah had looked through the side pane of the bay window and had been startled to see the couple sitting there. There was a silent pause on the mobile and Susannah thought she had lost the signal. "Hello?" she said. "Are you still there, Lindsay?"

"Yeah, stop messing, will you? Do you expect me to believe that?" Lindsay said, thinking her friend was winding her up.

She wasn't.

By the time Lindsay was on her way home, at around 5.30pm, the January skies had darkened. She got off the 79 bus and turned the corner into Rathbone Road.

When she reached her flat, she saw that the lamp was on, and felt quite relieved. It meant Peter was there. However, as Lindsay was disentangling her bunch of keys, ready to go into the flat, she saw movement out of the corner of her eye. She looked into the bay window and her heart almost stopped with fright. Two women, dressed in long black dresses and black high-collar jackets, were fighting - in her living room! Both women wore hats and one had her hands around the other's throat, and the much smaller woman was removing a long, lethal-looking hatpin from her hat. Lindsay watched, aghast, unable to comprehend what she was seeing.

The smaller woman repeatedly stabbed at the hands of the strangler with the pin, but although she hit her target every time, her efforts were to no avail, because her opponent was obviously in such a frenzy that she was oblivious to the hatpin plunging into her hand. Even when the smaller woman had become unconscious - or possibly dead - the strangler continued to shake her so violently that the little lady's hat fell off, and her hair, which had been arranged in a tight bun, fell out into curls as she went limp. Lindsay backed away from the window. Who the hell were these women? What was going on?

Without warning, the tall woman suddenly released her victim, who fell to the floor with a loud thud. The strangler then spun round to look directly at Lindsay, fixing her with a pair of the most prominent evil dark eyes. She then rushed across the living room - towards the door.

"Oh, my God!" shrieked Lindsay. "She's coming after me now!"

With that, she abandoned all ideas of letting herself into her flat and ran off down Rathbone Road. Without slowing, she looked back, expecting to see the outdated killer hot on her heels, but she saw instead only a present-day person walking towards her. This did little to reassure her and she carried on running, crossing the road to seek refuge at her Uncle Tyrone's house, on Long Lane. She told him what she had just witnessed and at first he suggested that Peter must have staged some sort of prank, but Lindsay called him on his mobile and he said he was with his brother in the Brookhouse pub, on Smithdown Road. She told him about the sinister-looking women in black and he thought she was joking, but said he would be home in about an hour.

Tyrone told her to stay put while he went and took a look for himself, but Lindsay insisted on going with him. When they entered the place, they found nothing amiss; no sign of any scuffle and certainly no sign of either of the belligerent women. Then Tyrone suddenly spotted something, "What's that?" he said and stooped down to pick up a long jewelled pin of some sort. It was more than likely the hatpin that Lindsay had seen the small woman stab her attacker with. That pin inexplicably vanished later that day.

The following day Lindsay visited her grandmother Irene, whose opinion she valued, to tell her about the strange incident, and Irene asked her if she had recently brought anything old into the flat, or altered it in any way.

"Well, yes, actually, now you come to mention it. Peter gave me this lovely old lamp and I've put it in the sitting room. He says it's an antique, but what's it got to do with what happened yesterday?"

Irene nodded her head knowingly. "Aha! It sounds like that might be the culprit. I've heard of this kind of thing before. Yeah, I bet it's that." And she advised Lindsay to remove the lamp from the flat immediately.

When Peter heard about the women in black, and Irene's belief that the lamp was somehow connected to them in a supernatural way, he felt a bit guilty for having introduced it into her life in the first place and suggested donating it to a charity shop as a way of diffusing the bad karma it had brought with it. Peter had a decent, honest friend named Ken who ran just such a charity shop, and a week after the lamp had been given to the shop, a middle aged woman came in and snapped it up, thinking she had got herself a real bargain. However, just five days later she returned it to the shop, plonking it down in front of the counter in disgust. She told Ken the lamp was haunted and she wanted her money back, and having got it, left without saying why she had come to that conclusion.

Three weeks passed before another customer, a man aged about fifty-five, came in and bought the Edwardian Bigelow and Kennard floor-lamp, but he too returned it after just three days. What he told Ken was, in turn, passed on to Peter. Apparently, on the third day after the new owner of the lamp had stood it in a corner of his living room, two ghosts appeared. The man was unable see them but his wife could, and she fainted at the sight of one of the ghosts trying to strangle the other one.

A few months went by, and one evening Ken and Peter were in a pub, when a young female student approached them, saying she recognised Ken as the man who ran the local charity shop. Ken nodded, and the girl, whose name was Kathy, told him that she and her flatmates lived near the shop, and most nights they had all seen the ghosts of two women appear in the shop around 11pm. The apparitions always vanished after one of them seemed to strangle the other one.

Her words struck an instant chord with Peter. Whoever had left that lamp in the empty house on Green Lane, was probably all too aware of its eerie reputation. He should never have stolen the object in the first place - it had brought nothing but grief.

The next day, Ken put out the lamp next to his wheelie bins for the refuse men to collect, but, it appears someone spotted it and robbed it before the binmen could take it away. The story behind the ghosts and the present whereabouts of the lamp are still unknown. Maybe it is still out there creating havoc for its present owner.

THE DAMNED

One grey October afternoon in the mid-1990s, Stephen Teabrook, who was then in his late twenties, was on his way up Hardman Street, having just left his flat on Rodney Street in order to go and browse at a bookshop called Atticus. He reached the narrow frontage of the bookshop, halted, and studied his reflection in the window for a moment, as he stood beside a life-sized wooden cut-out of the Irish expatriate writer, James Joyce. He had to admit that his reflection showed him up to be very scruffy and unkempt. He could not remember the last time he had had his wiry shoulder-length hair cut properly at a barbers - he usually had a chop at it himself, if he could be bothered -and now it sprouted sideways from beneath his homburg, and his dark calf-length coat looked dirty and worn.

Making a mental note to clean up his act, he turned his mind back to the present and with the little frisson of excitement that he always felt when he entered a bookshop, especially this one, which was his favourite, he went inside. Maybe it was the thrill of maybe finding that special book that no one else had got, or maybe it was just that womb-like quality of the place with its tall shelves packed close together. Whatever the reason, Stephen always felt comfortable and at home there. As soon as he set foot across the threshold, his ears were immediately assailed by the music of 'Mars, the Bringer of War' from Hoist's Planets Suite coming out of a radio tuned to Radio 3, hidden amongst the piles of books gathering dust somewhere behind the counter. The student sitting behind that counter was totally immersed in a copy of Harper Lee's *To Kill A Mockingbird*, oblivious to everything around him.

Stephen, having a life-long interest in the occult and matters of the paranormal, made straight for the Mind, Body and Spirit section of the shelves and started scanning them for books he had never come across before. He was soon to be rewarded when he spotted an early Fontana paperback edition of Capra's *The Tao of Physics*. He was eagerly thumbing through the yellowed pages when he suddenly remembered the interview at the Job Centre in Williamson Square for the Restart Course. Damn! He looked at his watch - 3.40pm! He should have been there seventy minutes ago, but surely they would not stop his benefit for genuine forgetfulness? He would ring them later with some excuse and hope for the best.

Stephen Teabook had now been on the dole for almost two years - ever since his break-up with his partner Penny. Since that split he had withdrawn from a cold inhospitable reality, into his comfy inner-world of the supernatural. He had cocooned himself within his vast collection of books on ghosts, the Tarot, astral travel, time travel, demons, real magic, Jungian psychology, Ouspensky, Crowley and Fortean phenomena. The dingy claustrophobic living room of his Rodney Street flat - which he referred to as his 'sanctum' - had dark wine-coloured walls adorned, amongst other things, with an eclectic mix of Buddhist Mandalas, an embroidered Seal of Solomon hanging mat, a gold-plated athame and a genuine Ngil tribal mask, said to have been used by African sorcerers.

In fact, Stephen's obsessive book-buying had been the principal cause of the split from Penny. They had taken over the flat, lining all four walls of the spare room, an entire wall of the living room, and had even found their way into the toilet, where Stephen had lined them up along the ledge over the cistern, with bits of toilet paper torn into makeshift bookmarks poking out of all of them.

After buying the Capra book, Stephen left Atticus, and with nothing better to do, decided he had better go and have a drink in the Philharmonic pub. He was heading in that direction when a familiar face approached. It was Chris Pound, a nasty little character who had once attended the same school as Stephen many years ago. He had been the classic school bully, pinching money and sweets from younger pupils and generally throwing his weight about. As an adult he was little better and nowadays was into all sorts of illegal money-making activities.

Pound slowed down and his huge shaved head tilted at an obtuse angle as he looked Stephen up and down. "Teabook? God, yer've put weight on!" he remarked with his usual bluntness, and he smiled for the briefest moment before his face reverted to its deadpan expression, except for the eyes, which continually darted about, making him look as shifty as he really was.

"Oh, hi, Chris," replied Stephen flatly, eager to get away from him.

"Hey, I've heard yer into witchcraft and all that sort of stuff, is that right?"

Stephen mumbled a vague reply and turned away, hoping to get rid of him, but Pound insisted on buying him a drink in the nearby Flying Picket pub. But there was no such thing as a free drink as far as Chris Pound was concerned, and Stephen knew perfectly well that he would have to repay the favour fourfold.

Inside the pub, he came out with a remarkable story. Howard, nicknamed 'Howie', a friend of his whom he described as an 'entrepreneur' - but in reality a habitual criminal, like himself - had just died. I am afraid that I cannot go into the shocking details of his death, but please take it for granted that this man did something unspeakably evil a year before he died, and the heinous act haunted him relentlessly till he passed away. Howie told the doctors, nurses, family and friends, indeed everyone who came to see him as he lay dying of a terrible disease in hospital, that 'they' were coming to get him to take him to Hell, as a punishment for something he had done. He said he had never been scared of death, but was terrified of going to Hell after he died.

A priest was called to help the troubled man and he told Howie not to worry, he would be forgiven as long as he repented his sins. But even after his visit, Howie complained that he was still suffering the most gruesome nightmares, in which demonic little things with red glowing eyes and sharp teeth invaded his coffin after his death. The priest gave up in the end, believing that Howie had a mental illness rather than a spiritual need.

A certain well-known local medium was sought out for advice after Howie had died, but was unable to help, and claimed that he was at rest, even though his body was seen to twitch in its open coffin whilst it was in his home, awaiting the funeral. Sickening sulphurous smells rose up from his corpse, and Howie's mother had even been woken up by her dead son's tormented screams at night. Now he was due to be buried in the morning and Chris Pound begged for Stephen's help. Normally he would have dismissed him as a low life, a loser, and wouldn't have given him the time of day, but he was the only person he knew with the kind of specialist knowledge he was looking for.

That evening, Chris Pound and a very reluctant Stephen, visited the home of the late man's mother. Stephen had tried to wriggle out of any involvement, but, just as in his schooldays, he felt powerless when up against Pound's overbearing personality and bullying tactics.

Howie's mother was a retired money lender, and like Howie she was a rough diamond - peroxide blonde hair, over-tanned skin like leather, gold rings on eight of her fingers, and a disgusting vocabulary of profanities. She was sobbing theatrically, face down on her sofa in the living room, as her two other sons looked on, lost for words. Chris winked at the sons as he and Stephen crept past the doorway of the living room, having explained to them earlier by telephone what he intended to achieve that night. So one of the sons closed the living room door as Chris and Stephen entered the parlour, in the middle of which lay the open coffin on its stand. Right away, Stephen's nostrils were assailed by the overpowering acidic odour in that room. His own flat didn't exactly smell of roses, but this was in a different league. It made his eyes water and he took a grubby handkerchief out of his pocket and coughed into it.

"Eh! Did yer see him move a bit then?" whispered Chris, staring at the corpse of his dead mate, which was dressed in a sharp royal blue suit, which must have made the undertakers smile when they saw it.

Stephen studied the corpse carefully - yes, the head definitely quivered slightly. He took a black leather-bound copy of the Holy Bible and placed it in the coffin, snugly between the corpse's right arm and the purple satin lining.

"Is that it?"

Chris was disappointed; at the very least he had expected Stephen to perform some esoteric rite involving chanting and perhaps burning a bit of incense or something. He could have stuffed a bible into the coffin himself.

"To be honest I don't think that'll help much -" Stephen replied, "- given what he did - he'll probably have to pay for what he did."

At this, the body rapidly sat up and opened its eyes - which were white and bulging. The jaw dropped open with a loud clacking sound out of the slack mouth came a long hiss. Hard man Chris immediately turned and ran out of the room, jabbering incoherently, unable to get his words out, but Stephen Teabook stood his ground. He calmly took an old crucifix from his inside pocket, then held it out to the evil being - or beings - that were occupying the dead body. Again, the response was rapid; the possessed corpse tossed the Bible out of the coffin and remained seated.

Stephen recited the Exorcism rite: "Evil spirit, I command you, in the name of God the Father Almighty, in the name of Jesus Christ his only son, and in the name of the Holy Spirit, that, harming no one, you depart from the body of this creature of God, and return to the place appointed to you in Hell, there to remain for eternity."

The eyes of Howie's corpse fell shut, but the body remained in a upright seated position for at least a minute, before it slowly sank back into the coffin. Stephen placed the Holy Bible back in the coffin, as Chris Pound peeped into the room accompanied by one of Howie's brothers. "What happened then. Ster" he enquired, nervously staring at the coffin.

"I think they've gone - for now, at least," Stephen told him. "Hopefully, they'll never possess this body again."

The next day during the funeral service, the coffin was placed on its bier in the middle of the church aisle. The priest intoned the solemn words he knew by heart, and as he did so, he and several members of the congregation became aware of a strange sound.

The corpse was kicking inside the coffin.

The priest was distracted a little by the unearthly sounds, and momentarily forgot where he was up to, but he dismissed them as someone in the congregation shuffling their feet. The mourners had heard it too and looked at one another with a mixture of fear and confusion. The pallbearers reported feeling the coffin jump about on their shoulders, as they carried it all the way to the grave. Howie's mother fainted at the graveside when she heard the dull sounds of her son crying in the coffin, as it was lowered into the clay. The gravediggers did their job as quickly as they could, and reported seeing the coffin shaking violently as they piled the soil on top of it. It needed three feet of soil to be shovelled on to the restless coffin, to eventually muffle the eerie sounds from the dead man.

When Howie's mother and brothers returned home, they found a smouldering black book in the middle of the floor in the front parlour. No title or words could be deciphered, as it was too badly burnt, but by the book's shape and size, they guessed it was almost certainly the copy of the Holy Bible that had been placed inside the coffin.

Everything that I have told you really took place. Funeral and burial lore is very old, and supernatural tradition dictates many strange things; that funerals always come in threes; that the first body to be interred in a new graveyard is claimed by the Devil, and that the last to be buried in a graveyard was destined to become the ghostly guardian of the cemetery until the 'Last Call' - the Day of Judgement.

In 1829, the first body was buried at St James's Cemetery, and as the coffin was committed to the earth, those attending the burial were fully aware of the superstition regarding the Devil claiming the first corpse to be interred in a cemetery. It is a matter of record that one of the worst thunderstorms to visit Liverpool in decades began to rage as the coffin was lowered into the beckoning grave and storms of a similar ferocity also raged when the last corpse was buried at the cemetery, in 1936.

As for the possession by evil spirits of a corpse in a coffin, it was an ancient tradition, mostly observed by the Celtic peoples, to have someone sit with the body with a lit candle nearby. This was done to discourage evil spirits from tormenting the soul of the deceased, as it took three days to fully separate from its earthly ties. Those attending a funeral are also at risk from deadly omens, according to this ancient lore. A ray of sunlight shining upon a particular mourner at a funeral means that that person is the next in line to die. Rain after a burial was said to be a good sign for the deceased, for it meant they had reached their destination in Heaven. Stephen Teabook is still investigating ghosts and performing exorcisms to this day.

THE DEVILS IN THE WINE CELLAR

Fear of ghosts and other supernatural entities - real or imagined - has often resulted in death by heart attack and stroke, in both young and old. A case in point was reported in the *Liverpool Mercury* newspaper for 15 November 1887. The article in that Victorian broadsheet reported that seven-year-old Southport child, Jane Halsall, died one night, believing that a terrible ghost from Liverpool was about to pay her a visit. Some children she had been playing with had apparently told her that the dreaded Spring-Heeled Jack (whom I have written about many times in my books) was coming to Southport after his scary antics in Liverpool.

Jane had taken this rumour to heart, and even though her mother tried to allay her fears by telling her that Jack was already "dead and buried", the little girl's vivid imagination got to work, and she became seriously ill and delirious in her bed that night. After rambling on about the jumping ghost from Liverpool for many hours, Jane lapsed into unconsciousness, never to awake again. The coroner, Mr Brighouse, officially recorded that the child's tragic death was due to 'congestion of the brain', which resulted in 'death from fright'.

One moonlit summer night, in 1979, the police were intrigued to catch sight of a youth named Paul, who had recently absconded from borstal, running up Moor Lane (the A565) from the direction of Ince Blundell. Paul had just abandoned a car he had stolen after colliding with a woman who had been standing in the middle of the road. When he pulled over and went back to see where she was, he expected to find her body in Moss Wood, which lies adjacent to the stretch of road where the accident had taken place. His speeding car had shuddered violently with the impact and he had cringed when he heard the sickening sound of her body slamming against the bonnet, as he shut his eyes. The force of the impact must surely have killed her and thrown her some distance from the car. Paul began a careful search of the roadside, dreading what he might find, but instead of finding an inert dead body in lying in the grass, he was confronted by a strangely dressed woman in a long dirty white gown, standing in the middle of the road in the moonlight. Her face wa unnaturally pallid, and where her eyes should have been there were cavernous black sockets.

She reached out towards the teenager, then, without any discernible movement from her legs or bare feet, she drifted steadily and silently towards him. The youth turned and fled back to the vehicle, with his legs wobbling like jelly, but as he tried to start the car, the ghostly woman in white entered the vehicle, her body passing through the rear of the car, and an icy hand grabbed the delinquent's mop of curly hair. He screamed, jumped out of the car and ran away as fast as he could. When he looked back, the phantom was still in pursuit of him with her arms outstretched.

When Paul saw the headlights of a car coming from the opposite direction, he ran instinctively straight towards them. It turned out that they belonged to a police patrol car, but he didn't mind running into the open arms of the law, indeed he felt safe now he was in their care. The runaway gave an incoherent account of the "woman in white" following him, but soon he had to stop when he became too breathless to speak. He was suffering from a full blown asthma attack.

Fortunately, two paramedics happened to be driving down nearby Scaffold Lane at that time and the police summoned their assistance by radio. Paul's asthma attack was successfully treated as the policemen in the patrol car drove up Moor Lane in search of the abandoned stolen car, which had its passenger door wide open. One of the policemen had already heard other accounts of the so-called Lady in White, who was alleged to haunt that stretch of road. Some thought she was the earthbound ghost of one of the many people who had either been run over, or crashed, at an infamous black spot on that road (which has a hazardous bend) years before.

In one such tragic instance, in June 2004, a mother and her two-year-old daughter and nine-year-old son died on that 'cursed' stretch of the A565, when the van they were travelling in careered off the road and smashed into a tree. It is said that not long after this tragedy, the Lady in White was once again on the prowl along the road close to the scene of the triple deaths.

In the early 1970s, there was a very strange case of supernatural beings possibly causing the death of a man through heart failure. The victim's friend suffered a stroke but survived to tell the weird tale. This story unfolds at a house on Second Avenue, Fazakerley, where a man named Alf and his friend Davy, both in their fifties, and both alcoholics, were staying, guests of a naive woman in her early sixties named Janet, who had taken pity on Alf and invited him to live with her a year before, and now bitterly regretted doing so, for every day he and his friend would get up, drink, go to town and drink again, and if they managed to make it back to her house, they would sit up for the remainder of the night drinking.

One day in the late winter of 1972, another drunk called at Janet's house bearing bad news. He told Alf that his forty-five-year-old sister, Marjorie, had died of natural causes as she slept in her bed. Although Marjorie had hated Alf with a vengeance, because of the disruption he had brought into her otherwise stable life, her brother broke down and cried when he heard the news - and he milked the bereavement to the maximum in order to obtain sympathy drinks in every pub he frequented across the region, from the Vines on Lime Street, to the Johnny Todd in Kirkby.

A month after the funeral, Alf's older brother, Vincent, suffered a heart attack and died at his house in Falkner Square. He was a cultured man who was as far removed from his drunken brother as the chimpanzee is to Stephen Hawking. For Janet, Vincent's death was a godsend, for his demise meant that Alf - as his only surviving next of kin - would inherit the house in Falkner Square, as well as seven thousand pounds - all that remained of Vincent's savings at the time of his death. Alf thanked Janet for looking after him and Davy, and at the beginning of March, after all of the forms had been signed and the will had been read, the solicitor completed the legal procedures and transactions, and Alf moved into his late brother's home before you could say Jack Robinson.

Janet burst into tears upon hearing of her lodgers' impending departure, and Alf hugged her, breathing his beery breath all over her and said, "There, there, love, you'll be okay." What he didn't realise was that they were tears of joy and relief, cried because Janet was so glad he was finally going and she could have her house back.

The Georgian house was finely furnished throughout and richly decorated, with expensive glittering crystal chandeliers and walls decked with original works of art, but it was all pearls before swine as far as the Philistine Alf was concerned. He poured himself a drink from a large tin of Watney's Party Seven ale into an expensive air-twist wine glass and toasted his late brother. "Nice one, our Vince! May you rest in peace."

"Yeah, I'll second that," laughed Davy, as he glugged down his usual glass of neat gin, "This is the life, old boy - what, what," and he and Alf settled back into their luxurious armchairs to enjoy a spy-fi action show called *Department S* on the huge colour television set.

The programme ended at 8.30pm, and Alf wandered off to take a look around his new home. He started in the cellar, where he made an exciting and very welcome discovery. Vincent had a well-stocked wine cellar. "Well, well, well," Alf laughed with glee, greedily eyeing the racks containing thousands of bottles of wine. "So my brother Vincent was a bit of a wine-squirrel."

Within the space of six months, Alf and Davy had made significant inroads into the wine, as part of their two-man mission to deplete the wine stock, and in addition to this, they were still also drinking their usual liquid diet of whisky, gin, vodka and bitter. Davy became ill at one point in this around-the-clock drinking marathon, and crawled on to the chesterfield sofa to sleep it off. Alf meanwhile, was rummaging around in the wine-cellar when he came upon a strange large bottle. Its size reminded him of the Long John whisky bottles that used to stand a few feet in length, only this one was made of dark red glass, and its top was covered in red sealing wax.

On the bottle's label was a symbol, which to Alf's permanently bloodshot eyes looked like the Star of David. If the description of this symbol (which was later given by Davy) is correct, then the star was actually the Seal of Solomon, an ancient occult symbol, often used as a talisman or amulet, and formed from two interlocking triangles. The Biblical King Solomon was said to possess a special ring of power which bore this seal, and oddly enough, the symbol of the six-pointed star had been stamped into the scarlet wax on the top of the tall red bottle.

Alf shook the bottle and put his eye up to the ruby-coloured glass. He thought he could see something floating around in it, but he couldn't make out what it was. He tried to remove the wax top, but it proved impossible, the seal would not budge, no matter how hard he twisted and turned it. He finally lost patience and swung the bottle at the bare brick wall of the cellar. As the glass smashed into the wall, there was an ear-splitting explosion, and a cloud of red smoke rapidly expanded from the point of impact. Soon a pink mist had filled the cellar, and it brought with it a sweet but sickly aroma.

Alf was scratching his head in disbelief at all this when a familiar silhouette appeared at the top of the cellar steps. It was Davy. The noise of the explosion had roused him from his drunken stupor and he had come down to find out what had caused it. He saw the reddish smoke coming from the shattered remains of the bottle, which still had its label intact. Suddenly, three small bright lights with faint reddish halos came fizzing and buzzing through the smoky air. As Alf was gasping out, "What are they?" the lights flew straight for him, and he let out a yelp of agony and fell down on the stone floor of the cellar.

"Alf! Are you alright, mate? Alf -!"

Davy wafted the pink smoke out of the way as he rushed across the cellar to pick up his friend, who was now shrieking in pain. As he got nearer to him Davy saw something very sinister and surreal - the three hovering lights were actually little red glowing creatures of some sort, and as they darted about they made an alarming buzzing sound like a hornet, only much louder.

Alf cried out in pain as he tried to get back up on his feet. Two of the lights were still frantically circling his head, and cuts and slashes were appearing all over the drunk's face. The other luminous creature suddenly flew at Davy, and as it got nearer, he could see that it was some kind of insect, about six centimetres in length, with long angular arms and legs similar to a preying mantis, only it had a tail with a triangular point at the end, and a pair of wings that were just a phosphorescent blur. On its head there were two pointed appendages that looked like horns. The black beady eyes of this thing were firmly fixed on Davy, and he turned and ran back up the cellar steps, abandoning Alf to his fate.

As Davy was halfway back up the cellar steps, he felt a sharp stinging sensation in the back of his neck, and when he turned round, he saw that it had been inflicted by one of the horned glowing 'devils' hovering close by him at face level. Its black lifeless doll-like eyes and grimacing fanged mouth conveyed an impression of utter malice. Davy left the cellar and ran through the hall towards the vestibule door, and there he collapsed. He woke up in hospital, unable to move his left-sided limbs, and was told he had suffered a stroke. He also learned from his sister that Alf was dead. He had been found on the cellar floor, having died from what appeared to have been a massive heart attack. The scratches on his face were assumed to have been made by the glass fragments from the smashed red bottle which was found near his body.

Davy knew better, and despite misgivings about not being believed, he gave his strange account of the little 'devils' who had attacked him and his friend. The specialist just smiled. He obviously thought the glowing creatures were figments of a brain pickled in alcohol, not to mention the stroke he had suffered. Yet Davy clearly remembered the symbol on the bottle's label and he even got a relative of Alf's to retrieve the label as well as the wax top of that mysterious bottle.

If we are to believe Davy's story, what are we to make of the little devilish insect-type creatures? Were they, as the story seems to suggest, some supernatural phenomenon, and had they been confined by some occultist to the red bottle with the seals of Solomon upon it?

LITTLE DEVILS

A Mrs Daintry wrote to me in 1997 to tell me of a strange story that has a striking parallel with the last tale. In the summer of 1964, Mrs Daintry's forty-four-year-old sister, Annie Green, went to have a back tooth extracted by a dentist named Savitz, at his surgery on Kirkdale's Walton Road. The extraction was relatively painless, thanks to just the right amount of local anaesthetic being professionally administered and Annie returned home to her house on Freeland Street feeling glad to be rid of the troublesome molar. She had been told to take it easy for the rest of the day, to prevent complications and allow herself to recover from the anaesthetic, so she went straight into the parlour as soon as she got home and listened to the radio and relaxed in her armchair. Annie's fourteen-year-old daughter Susan offered to go fetch the *Liverpool Echo* and some groceries at the local shops for her mum.

While Susan was out on the errand, Mrs Green held her palm to the side of her mouth to feel the swelling in her numbed jaw. She then dozed off for a few minutes, and when she awoke she ran her tongue around her mouth, shuddering slightly at the metallic taste of the clotted blood. She decided to swill the clots from her gums with a glass of water, and as she got up to go to the kitchen, her attention was caught by a loud humming sound out in the hallway. Annie Green had a phobia of wasps and bees, and for a moment she thought the humming heralded the arrival of some hornet or bumble-bee that had flown into the house via the half-open kitchen window. But then the source of the buzzing came down the hallway and flew in a curve towards the parlour doorway: a little red devil, about four inches tall. It looked just like a miniature human male, with crimson skin and a pointed tail. Mrs Green turned and bolted back into the parlour and she slammed the door behind her, just in the nick of time.

She tried to make sense of what she had just seen. Could the anaesthetic - albeit only a local one - have had some affect on her mind? Then she heard the buzzing sound coming close up to the door, and a faint but frantic rapping sound on the other side, as if it were trying to force its way in. Mrs Green was not a churchgoer, and neither was she in any way a religious person, but she felt impelled to make the sign of the cross, because she sensed that the winged creature in the hallway had something to do with the Devil. She then heard another humming sound, at a slightly different pitch, that was growing in intensity in the hallway. With dread, she realised that another one of those satanic things had invaded her home.

The unearthly little beings tapped away persistently at the parlour door, and Mrs Green bashed the door with her fist, hoping the thuds would scare them off, but the humming sounds of the surreal flying imps merely increased in intensity and they continued to tap furiously on the door. Then the rapping noises stopped for a tense moment, only to be replaced soon after by a scraping sound, as if something with a sharp point was being scored into the door. She looked around frantically for something with which to strike the weird visitants and made a grab for the curved brass poker that was resting on the coal fire's fender. It was certainly heavy enough, but it was much too thin; she would probably miss the little red fiends if she tried to swipe them with it.

On the radiogram in the corner there rested a large heavy leather-bound copy of the Holy Bible, which Mrs Green's neighbour had lent to her some months previously. She was actually rather embarrassed about it because, as yet, she had not even turned a page of it. However, she judged it to be just about the right width to swat the sinister trolls. At that moment, Susan passed the parlour window on her return from the shops, so Mrs Green dashed across and opened the top side window. "Susan, wait there!" she shouted to her daughter, who was standing on the doorstep with the heavy bag of groceries and the *Echo* rolled up in her fist.

"What, mum?"

"Just wait there!"

Mrs Green picked up the Bible and opened the door a fraction to find that now only one of the tiny red figures was hovering there. It made a high-pitched hum and a simultaneous droning sound, as it darted straight towards the Liverpool housewife. She was primed for action and swung the heavy Bible at it, whacking its diminutive body with considerable force. The thing was knocked clean out of the air and landed in the hallway, its limbs disjointed and broken-looking, as it lay motionless on the floor. Now that she was able to study it more closely, she saw that there was definitely something insect-like about it.

Susan got tired of waiting outside and chose to disobey her mother's instruction and let herself in with her key. As she stepped into the hall, she was met by the sight of her mother, holding the Bible ready to strike again, should the thing which was wriggling on the floor come back to life.

"What's that, Mum?" Susan, asked, startling her mother. The tiny red winged creature had suddenly recovered from the wallop, and was now rotating in a tight circle on its side, its wings flapping at a phenomenal speed. Susan screamed and dropped the groceries as she recoiled in fright, her eyes fixed on the 'devil'. Mrs Green stepped in front of her, shielding her from the minuscule demon. The thing suddenly righted itself and took off, and mother and daughter let out a scream as it flew past them and out through the open front door and into the street. A mongrel dog bounded past, growling, and when Susan and her mother went outside, they watched as the animal chased the red spot that was flying in a haphazard zigzag pattern up the length of Freeland Street.

Of course, no one believed their story about the little red devil, and when Mr Green came home and his wife showed him the marks clawed by the two devils into the parlour door, he still could not accept the weird tale. Mrs Green started fretting about the other little winged man she had seen, and for years she would go cold whenever she heard the innocent humming of a mundane bee or wasp that had got trapped in the house.

Some days after the little devils had menaced the

Kirkdale woman at her home on Freeland Street, hundreds of people across the Northwest reported seeing the 'Little People'. The *Liverpool Echo*, on the 2 July 1964, reported that scores of people had seen 'Leprechauns' on the bowling green near Jubilee Drive, in Kensington. Other strange pixie-like beings were seen in the grounds of Liverpool University, off Oxford Street, and 'fairies' were also sighted and chased in Princes Park, Sefton Park, Newsham Park, Birkenhead Park, Stanley Park, the grounds of St Chad's Church in Kirkby, as well as many other parts of the region. Mass mania was blamed, and then a UFO sighting that came in from a lady in Crosby on the eve of the Kensington 'Leprechaun' sightings provided another possibility to those with open minds - that the Little People being seen across the North West were extraterrestrial in origin. The sightings soon died down and the whole strange affair was gradually forgotten.

Was it only a case of mass psychosis or, did miniature alien or supernatural beings, including the little red devils of Freeland Street, really invade that quantum of fuzzy perceptions we call reality?

CROSSED LINE

If you were about to make a telephone call from a landline or a mobile, and you heard two people having a conversation, would you quickly hang up, or would you be tempted to listen in? Curiosity is a powerful state of mind, and when twenty-one-year-old Gateacre girl Lisa picked up her mother's telephone handset one rainy afternoon in the early 1980s, in order to make a call to a friend, she heard female voices, slightly distorted, on the line, with a buzzing sound in the background. Lisa placed her hand over the mouthpiece and listened intently. She knew it was wrong to eavesdrop, but she could not help herself. One voice sounded young, probably around her own age and the other sounded as if the speaker was about sixteen. Before an interruption occurred, this was how the snatch of conversation went:

"Are you telling me you're pregnant?"

"Yeah."

"Have you been the doctor's and that?"

"Yeah, I went yesterday (sobbing) - what am I going to do?"

"Just go home -"

"I can't, my dad will kill me."

"Course he won't, look - meet me at the shopping

centre."

"Where?"

"Belle Vale Shopping Centre -"

The buzzing sound grew louder, swamping out the voices, and as Lisa strained to listen, her mother came up and asked, "Who's that you're talking to?"

Lisa raised her palm to her mother and said, "Sshh! Wait a minute, Mum."

"Hey, don't shush me, Lisa," said her mother, annoyed. "It is my phone you know!"

The line suddenly went deathly quiet, and Lisa reluctantly put the handset down. She picked it up off the cradle again and listened once more, just in case she got the same crossed line, but it was just the familiar electronic purring tone and she turned to her mother and told her what she had just heard.

"You nosy mare," said Lisa's mum. How would you like people listening in to your conversations?" Then she had an unnerving afterthought, "Hey, if we can hear strangers talking on our line, d'you think they've been listening in to our conversations? I don't like that idea. I'll phone the telephone fellah later and ask him."

Lisa's mother worked as a dinner lady in the local school, and she was worried that some eavesdropper might have heard her gossiping about a certain colleague she worked with when she was on the phone to her friend.

"I wonder who it is that's having a baby. She only sounded like a schoolgirl - poor thing." Lisa sat down on the sofa and started sucking the very tip of her thumb - a habit her mother hated with a vengeance. Lisa always reverted to it whenever she was deep in thought and was barely aware that she was doing it.

"You need to mind your own business, Lisa. It's got nothing to do with you."

Her mum switched on the television and started watching a children's programme called *Ragdolly Anna*, just for the sake of something to watch, because there was nothing else of interest on at that time in the afternoon. Lisa meanwhile, was back at the telephone, dialling her friend Valerie's number, who lived on the Belle Vale estate. She told her about the 'crossed line' and how she had overheard a girl who sounded as if she was just in her teens saying she was pregnant. "It must be someone around your end, because they mentioned meeting at Belle Vale Shopping Centre."

On the following day, which was a Tuesday, Lisa went off to college at 9.30am. She was studying economics and book-keeping - though in a very half-hearted way - because she had made the wrong choice and was finding the subjects very boring. What she really wanted to do was become a hairdresser. When she returned home at half-past two, she told her mother, who had just returned from her shift at the school dinner centre, that she no longer wanted to become an accountant. "I want to open my own hairdressing salon in town, or maybe Chester," she told her mother, who was becoming rather irritated at the way her daughter was constantly changing her mind. "My friend's doing hairdressing and she says it's great."

"Oh, Lisa, why don't you just go and live on Cloud Nine?"

"I *knew* you'd say that. You never listen to me."

"Well, it's one fad after another with you. You never settle down to anything."

"That's right, make me feel like a complete failure. You never encourage me, do you? You've some need to talk - no wonder you're just a dinner lady! Don't dare rise above your station - know your place, Mum! You should listen to yourself, you're pathetic!"

With that, Lisa threw down her slim blue ring-binder of college work and flounced into the hallway to grab her coat. She slammed the front door behind her and was in such a huff, stomped all the way to Valerie's home on the Belle Vale estate, without realising that the dark coat she had on was not hers, but her mother's. She only found out when she felt her mother's purse in the pocket.

Lisa sat at the glass-topped table in Valerie's kitchen, where the two girls chatted and dreamed of unlikely futures. Valerie complained that she had had the same trouble with both her parents; they seemed to be hell bent on destroying her dreams and crushing her self confidence. Her dad had laughed at her and said she was too fat when she said she wanted to be an air stewardess, and when Valerie had proposed sending a demo tape of songs she had written to EMI, her mother also laughed her to scorn, saying she had no chance, thereby shattering what little confidence she had left. Their idea of a suitable career for their daughter only stretched so far as to urge her to go and work at the Jacob's biscuit factory in Aintree.

Late in the afternoon the two girls went to the Highwayman public house and carried on grumbling about their parents and wistfully discussing their unachievable goals over a few glasses of lager and lime. By 6.30pm, Lisa had done a foolhardy thing; she had 'borrowed' money from her mother's purse, and it was money she would have a very hard time replacing, because her only source of income was supplementary benefit, and she had already spent up her allowance for the week. "If I were you I'd just spend her money and then go to the police and say you lost her purse," Val suggested.

"I can't rob off my own mother and then lie to her as well," Lisa replied, with tears in her eyes. "What do you take me for?"

That evening, Lisa was too scared to face her mother, and decided to stay over at Valerie's. At 8pm, Valerie showed Lisa her new outfit - purchased from a mail-order catalogue, and Lisa instantly fell in love with it. She tried it on and it immediately made her want to hit the town for a night out - paid for with her mother's money. As the two girls put on their make-up and styled and straightened their hair, Debbie, Valerie's fifteen-year-old cousin, poked her head round the door.

"Ooh! You two look really lovely," she said, and then she asked Val if she could go out with them. Valerie said she couldn't, because she was underage, but Debbie tried to persuade her by arguing that she would look much older when she had got dressed up and done her make-up.

"That band - Afraid of Mice - are on at Plummers tonight," she told the older girls, her eyes sparkling with excitement. "Go on - please let me come. I won't be a nuisance, honest."

Val and Lisa looked at one another with expressions of pure empathy towards the girl. They remembered how desperate to get out they had been at fifteen and so they both caved in and said they'd take a chance and let her go out with them. "But you'd better behave, or this'll be the last time."

Debbie was over the moon.

At 9pm the three girls were riding the bus into town, and they then headed straight to a certain club in the city centre where Lisa and Val distracted the doorman's attention by flirting with him, whilst Debbie sneaked into the premises. So far so good, but then, at half-past eleven, Debbie went missing from the club. The girls became frantic and searched everywhere for her. A doorman said he had seen her leave with a man a few years older than herself at around 11.15pm. There was nothing more that they could do and so they returned home, hoping to find Debbie waiting for them, but unfortunately that was not the case.

Lisa stayed at Val's that night, and now had two major worries - the disappearance of young Debbie, and the spending of nearly all of her mother's purse money. All she had left out of fifty pounds was a ten-pound note; her mother would go mad. Debbie finally turned up in tears at her cousin's home at three o'clock in the morning. She apologised for leaving the club without telling them, but she had bumped into a lad she had fancied at school. His name was Rob and he was three years older than her. He had taken her to a friend's house and had unprotected sex with her. This shocking bit of news just about crowned that horrendous twenty-four hours.

At breakfast the following morning, Valerie's father overheard Lisa saying she urgently needed forty pounds to put back in her mother's purse.

"What's that? Been pinching money out of your

mum's purse, have you?"

"I didn't mean to - I put my mum's coat on by mistake last night and it just sort of happened."

"Well, you're in shit street, aren't you?"

"You're not kidding. My mum will go ballistic when she finds out. How am I going to tell her?"

"Well, I might just have an idea that could help you out," said Val's dad. "If it fails, you'd lose the ten pounds you've still got left and, okay, you'd be in an even worse predicament, but if it works, you'll get you forty quid, plus a few bob for yourself.

"So what's the idea?" asked Lisa, cautious, but interested.

"There's a horse running today at Redcar -"

"Oh! Here we go!" said Val. "I might have known that would be the best you could come up with, Dad. Just ignore him Lisa, you'll end up as skint as he is."

"No, listen. It's running in the Dunsdale Stakes. With odds of six to one, we could make sixty quid, plus our stake back, if it comes in; that's if we stick a tenner on it."

"Well, I suppose I've got nothing to lose - in for a penny, in for a pound, or however the saying goes."

"But, Lisa -" put in Val. "What if -"

"Look, Val, I know what you're saying, but I might as well give it a go. Mum'll be almost as mad whether I just give her the tenner, or I say the lot's gone."

"Okay, it's your money - well that's not quite true, but -" and the two girls fell about laughing.

Lisa handed Val's dad the ten pounds, and he put it on a horse called Tubes Care, ridden by a jockey called Seagrave. It turned out to be a good move, because the horse won, and he collected the seventy pounds. He gave Lisa fifty-five and kept fifteen for himself, which meant she could now go back home with her conscience cleared and without fear of retribution. She apologised to her mother for storming out the night before and for all the nasty things she had said, but Lisa's mum already knew that her daughter had not meant any of it.

Lisa became friendly with Debbie after that disastrous night, and strongly advised the girl never to sleep with anyone again, until she was old enough to look after herself better. Debbie looked up to Lisa like an older sister, and was always telephoning her for advice. One afternoon she rang Lisa, and something remarkable happened. Debbie confided that she had started throwing up each morning before she went to school. She also told her that, as from today, she was staying at a friend's house in Childwall, and' she was never going back home.

"Are you telling me you're pregnant?"

As the words came out of her mouth, Lisa felt a faint sensation of *deja vu*. She had heard that line before somewhere, but she couldn't quite place it.

"Yeah," was Debbie's stark reply.

Then, with butterflies in her stomach, Lisa recalled the crossed line conversation she had overheard months before. "Have you been the doctor's and that?"

"Yeah, I went yesterday," Debbie sobbed. "What am I going to do?"

Lisa implored the young teenager to do the sensible thing, "Just go home -"

"I can't, my dad will kill me," Debbie told her and burst into tears.

Lisa had to think fast before Debbie hung up. "He won't, look - meet me at the shopping centre."

"Where?"

"Belle Vale Shopping Centre -"

Debbie hung up.

Lisa told her mother what had happened, and asked her if she recalled the crossed line incident a few months ago.

"Yes, as a matter of fact I do, love," her mum replied. "Isn't that strange? Maybe it was meant to be some kind of warning or something."

In the event, Debbie miscarried the baby, but she had learned her lesson as far as men like Rob were concerned and wisely waited until she was a lot older before she had another serious relationship. But that is not the end of this uncanny story. A few months after Debbie's miscarriage, Lisa picked up the telephone one evening at around 10pm, intending to call Val, but before she could even dial her friend's number, she heard voices on the line. She went cold. Despite the faint background hum, Lisa recognised one of the voices only too well, because it belonged to herself. She put her hand over the telephone mouthpiece and listened as her heart raced. What she heard shocked her to her very core, because the voice went on to say, "The funeral's on Monday."

An unknown female voice then said, "Lisa, are you sure you're okay? Do you want to stay over at ours tonight?"

Lisa slammed the handset down into its cradle. She didn't want to hear any more. She never told her mother about it because she was convinced that the funeral she had heard about would be her mother's.

For many years Lisa lived in dread of the awful premonition coming true, but her mother is still going strong, and at the time of writing is in her late seventies. Lisa became so worried by the weird telephonic phenomenon, she went to see a priest at one point, and he told her to pay no attention to the voices, for he believed that they were the work of the Devil.

Perhaps the whole thing was simply a genuine crossed lined and just a lot of coincidence, but if you hear voices on your telephone as you're about to make a call, perhaps it's best to hang up.

THE RED MENACE

At book-signings, or after illustrated talks on the paranormal I have presented, people have often come up to me and told me about a certain supernatural character. I have also learned more about his sinister antics through letters, emails, and sometimes from listeners to radio shows on which I have appeared as a guest. All of these stories seem to dovetail into one another to create the impression that there may be a weird, inhuman prowler at large in Liverpool, operating mostly on nights of the full moon. This person never ages, and has, if the stories are to be believed, been around for many decades. Furthermore, he is seemingly still going strong today.

The earliest report I have of this bogeyman dates back to 1967. That year, on the Tuesday night of 23 May, there was a full moon. Dawn Whittaker had recently turned fifteen years of age, and on this moonlit night, at half-past ten, she and her school friend Nancy were sitting on a sofa, engrossed in an episode of *The Forsyte Saga*. Dawn's five-year-old brother Malcolm was sprawled across the floor, playing with his Lego bricks. He asked his sister where his mummy had gone, and without taking her attention from the screen, she told him that mummy and daddy were at a party and would be back later.

Then Malcolm went into the kitchen and hurled the rather wonky Lego plane he had just constructed into a sink full of dishes, cups and cutlery that should have been washed up hours ago. At 11.15pm when the Forsyte Saga ended, Dawn decided to go and make some cheese on toast, and she found Malcolm standing on the draining board next to the sink, looking in fascination at the tap, which was gushing into a bowl full of foam and washing-up. He had squeezed a considerable quantity of washing-up liquid into the bowl, and was enjoying the froth of the bubbles swelling up from the sink.

"Malcolm! What have you done?" cried Dawn. She wanted to shout at him but her sleepy little brother looked so cute sitting on the drain board, watching the mess he had caused, that she didn't have the heart to do it.

Nancy came in and when she saw the chaos Malcolm was causing in the sink, said, "Dawn, he should have been put to bed hours ago. Your mum and dad will go mad when they see him still up - not to mention all this mess he's made."

"Oh, he's alright, aren't you, Male? And we can soon get this lot sorted out after we've had our cheese on toast."

Having no ventilation grille in the kitchen, Dawn opened the kitchen window and lit the gas jets of the cooker's toaster with a Swan Vesta match. The family had no fridge, and so Dawn went to get the cheese and bread from the larder, which led off the hallway, and Nancy followed her. Seconds after leaving the kitchen they heard Malcolm let out a terrific scream. The girls looked at one another in shock for a heart-stopping moment then ran back into the kitchen to find Malcolm being dragged out of the kitchen through the ten-inch gap in the window. His little legs were kicking violently in protest as he was being pulled slowly out into the night. Dawn grabbed at one of his legs and the top of his shorts and tried to pull him back in, but someone with great strength was pulling him away from her. She saw what looked like a "dark red hand" with long tapering fingers around the boy's waist, digging deep into his flesh. Malcolm, by this time, was screaming hysterically. Nancy grabbed hold of the toddler's other leg and a desperate tug of war ensued between the unseen baby snatcher and the teenaged girls. Dawn climbed up on to the draining board and pulled at her baby brother with all her might, and suddenly she managed to yank him back through the window, albeit minus his pullover. The would-be kidnapper had pulled it off.

Dawn cradled her crying brother in her arms and tried to calm him, as Nancy climbed up on to the window ledge and looked out through the gap at the backyard of the St Domingo Vale house. It was silvered by the moon's light, but Nancy could see no one outside and heard no sounds of anyone running away - so she assumed that the man who had tried to make off with Malcolm was still hiding somewhere close by and probably watching her, and that possibility froze her blood. The window was slammed shut and the lights switched on in every room. Nancy bolted the front door and then sat down with Dawn on the sofa, with Malcolm sandwiched in between them, still crying, and asking if that "very bad man" had gone. Dawn asked him if he had recognised the man who had tried to take him and he shook his head, crying out again and asking for his mother. There was no telephone in the house and so Dawn had no way of contacting the police and she and Nancy just had to sit tight until her parents returned.

The tense atmosphere in the house was even further heightened that night when a programme, entitled *The Witches of Alderley Edge* - about witchcraft and supernatural goings-on in Cheshire - came on the television. At around half-past one, Dawn's parents returned from the party, and the girls told them about the attempted abduction of little Malcolm, who was now scrambling up his mother in tears. Dawn's father, Harry, put his own interpretation on their account of the kidnap, arguing that the abductor was probably just "that weird lad" - a fourteen-year-old problem child named Mick, who lived in the next street. Nancy soon discounted that theory when she told him that Mick, who lived next door to her, was in Wales on holiday with his older brother that night and so could not have been responsible. All the same, Dawn's parents failed to take the attempted abduction of Malcolm as seriously as they should have done.

Late that night, Dawn's father walked Nancy home to the next street. The girl was on obviously on edge and kept on glancing nervously about; the full moon's eerie light conjuring up all kinds of bogeymen in her imagination. When Harry returned, he first gave Dawn a good telling off for not having done the dishes and letting Malcolm stay up so late and then told her to get to bed. He was very disappointed. She went up to her room, feeling bad about letting her parents and her little brother down but found she couldn't sleep. She could hear Malcolm still crying next door, which filled her with guilt. After all, she was supposed to have been looking after him that night and she had not done a very good job. He was sleeping with his parents because he had been reduced to a nervous wreck, and would have nightmares about the stranger trying to snatch him for weeks afterwards.

At around three o'clock that morning, Dawn dozed off for a few minutes, but no sooner had she fallen asleep than a noise awakened her. She could not say how she knew, but she was certain that someone was watching her through the gap where her heavy thick curtains failed to meet. She slowly got out of bed, and as she crept across the floor, she heard a faint sound outside. She froze and listened. Silence for a while - and then a motorcycle passing through the neighbourhood, somewhere in the distance.

Having reached the curtains, she slowly parted them, but only about an inch - to be confronted by a pair of eyes looking back at her through the window. The rest of the face looked very dark - almost mulberry coloured - and that unnatural colour, coupled with the fact that the peeping tom was at a first-floor window that was at least twenty feet off the ground, caused Dawn to let out a shrill cry. The man instantly dropped from the window and there was a soft thud in the street below, followed by the faint padding of someone nimble-footed running off into the darkness.

Dawn burst into her parents' room, awakening poor Malcolm, who had been through enough that night already. Dawn's mother was out cold from all that drinking at the party, and she had to shake her snoring father three or four times before he grunted in annoyance and begrudgingly opened one eye. He was furious at her seemingly farfetched account of the "dark red" man at the window, and at the top of his voice he told his daughter to "grow up". All the screaming and shouting started Malcolm off again and he was soon howling the house down, and patting his mum's sleeping face to wake her up.

Dawn stormed angrily back to her room, slamming the door, and throwing the curtains wide open. By this time her fear had turned to anger and she was hoping to see the weird prowler, because she wanted to punch him for making her seem like a crackpot in front of her parents, but she saw nothing but the moonlit backyards and rooftops. Not a living thing stirred in that static nightscape, not even the usual alley cat that could be seen roaming the tops of the walls most nights. The next day, Dawn told Nancy what she had seen, and her friend said they should stay up late and see if the bizarre-looking stranger turned up again. Dawn asked her mother if Nancy could stay over, and her mother said she didn't mind, but Dawn's dad put his foot down and said no. He didn't want a repeat of the hysterics of the night before, with the girls staying up all night, and terrifying Malcolm. But the girls had other ideas! Dawn told Nancy to leave her own house at around one o'clock in the morning and go down the entry. "I'll be watching from my window, and I'll go down and let you in through the backyard gate."

"Hold on a minute, what if that nutter's out there lurking in the alley," protested Nancy. "He might grab me like he did your Malc."

"I told you, I'll be watching. You'll be fine."

Nancy was reluctant to go ahead with Dawn's

harebrained scheme, but her friend somehow managed to talk her into it in the end.

Just after one in the morning, Nancy sneaked out of her house, pulling the front door to as softly as she could. She stared at the eastern sky over the rooftops. The moon looked as if it was still full, but it was in fact now just past its full phase and on the wane, yet its lunar radiance still lent a spooky aspect to the neighbourhood, and transformed inanimate objects which, by day, would not evoke a second glance, into menacing entities of the peripheral vision.

Nancy hurried along the street, keeping her wits about her all the time, and then crept down the alleyway. She was stopped in her tracks by a large black Alsatian dog, which stood there, facing the other way, as it growled at a stray cat, with its back arched and its fur standing on end, perched on a backyard wall. The girl was terrified of dogs, and she quickly backed away and expected the dog to come after her, but the Alsatian was obviously too spellbound by its feline opponent to have noticed her and the stand off continued.

So Nancy was forced to go the long way round to Dawn's, and that meant venturing into the dark end of the street, where one of the lamp-posts was always out of action for some reason. Recently there had been a spate of break-ins down this end of the street, and some believed it was the burglars who were deliberately smashing the lamp-post bulbs in order to facilitate their night-work.

A strong sweet smell hung in the lukewarm air that night, and it became more and more pungent as Nancy approached the mouth of the alleyway. She passed a dustbin, and imagined that the unusual scent was coming from that, but when she lifted the lid, the bin was empty. Then what was that? She heard a noise somewhere in the alley. She shot a look behind, but there was no one there. She broke into a trot, and the sound of her footsteps set a fierce-sounding dog barking furiously behind one of the backyard gates. Its barks set off another yard dog further down the alley, and that in turn set another hound howling. She must have inadvertently woken half the neighbourhood.

In the middle of this nocturnal cacophony, Nancy happened to glance over her right shoulder to glimpse the shadow of a man on top of the alley wall - a silhouetted figure in tight-fitting clothes, running alongside her - only he was running with a remarkable sense of balance along the narrow backyard walls. Nancy went numb with fear and found she couldn't breathe properly, never mind cry out. She did not look up again, because she hoped the man had not noticed her noticing him, and she believed he might just give up the chase.

She finally reached the backyard gate to Dawn's house, but Dawn was expecting her to come from the other direction, and so was looking the wrong way, and failed to notice her friend. Nancy desperately tried to open the wooden gate but the bolt was on, so she knocked several times on it, and luckily for her, Dawn heard her and came down to let her in. Those few minutes, as Nancy stood waiting for her friend to let her into the yard, were the most terrifying minutes of her life. The backyard door opened, and a terrified Nancy was still unable to speak - but Dawn didn't even seem to notice. "Guess what I got from Cousins today for me and you?" she whispered with a smile and she closed the yard gate and bolted it as Nancy followed her uneasily to the kitchen door. "I got us a whole sandwich cake - you like them don't you, Nance? And I made some corned beef sarnies as well."

To her, this was just another sleepover - a bit of fun - with maybe a bit of adventure thrown in, should they see the weird stranger once again.

It was only when the two girls were inside the kitchen, that Dawn suddenly noticed that her friend was speechless and shaking like a leaf, and she asked her what was wrong. When Nancy revealed that a shadowy man had run along the tops of the backyard walls, following her, Dawn went cold. Having first made sure the kitchen door was bolted, she then took Nancy upstairs to her room and carefully closed the door behind her, so as not to awaken the rest of the household.

Lying on the bed, under the glow of a lamp on the bedside cabinet, was a folded pink and white gingham tablecloth, and upon that, there was the promised sandwich cake from the confectioners on Oakfield Road, which Dawn, in a thoughtful mood, had bought earlier in the day with her babysitting money. On the next plate there were four corned beef sandwiches, and two bottles of orange-flavoured 'Zing', Dawn's favourite soft drink.

The girls tucked into their nocturnal feast, and by two in the morning, Nancy had calmed down and had even begun to try and think of a rational explanation for the man running along the wall. She was aware, like the rest of the neighbourhood, that there had been a number of break-ins round there recently, so perhaps the wall walker was a burglar casing one of the houses, rather than anything more sinister? That seemed a very weak explanation to Dawn. Burglars usually kept a very low profile and stayed in the shadows; they certainly didn't run along backyard walls to attract people's attention and risk breaking their necks in the process.

Just after two, there was movement on the landing outside Dawn's bedroom. It was only her father, getting up to go to the toilet. The bedside lamp was promptly switched off and neither girl said a word while they could still see the landing light shining under the bedroom door. As soon as Dawn's father had returned to his bedroom and closed the door behind him, the girls started chatting again, but instead of putting the lamp back on, Dawn opened the curtains to allow the bright moonlight to flood the room. She then lifted open her sash window by about eight inches.

A few minutes later, something startling happened. A black and white police panda car came tearing down the road outside. It decelerated abruptly and came to a halt outside of Dawn's house, then quickly reversed up the road again. The weird-looking man in the skin-tight clothing then came hurtling down the street, from the direction of the panda car. Passing under a lamp-post, Dawn and Nancy caught a glimpse of him and what they saw made them shudder. He had a prominent straight nose, a thick head of dark hair that sprouted straight up, and was wearing a pale tee shirt, skin-tight dark blue trousers and possibly black plimsolls. In that brief moment, they also noticed that his face and forearms were of an unnatural reddish colour, and Dawn immediately made the connection with the dark red hand around Malcolm's waist as he was being pulled out of the kitchen window - and the red face she had seen at her window the night before.

Dawn and Nancy leaned out and watched as two young policemen ran after the weird red-skinned man, but he effortlessly outran the officers of the law, soon putting a phenomenal distance between himself and his pursuers, and then the teenaged girls both gasped in astonishment as they watched the distant silhouette of the fleeing figure run vertically up a wall, only to vanish into the darkness.

This last apparent ability to run up vertical surfaces is one of the 'impossible' traits of the prowler that is found in every account I have heard, or read about him. The police must have accepted that they were no match for the hyper-agile visitor, because they quickly gave up their pursuit. Dawn and Nancy, however, were still curious and doggedly kept up their moonlight vigil. Nancy put her empty bottle of Zing on the window sill and stuck her head out into the cool night air. It was just after 3am, and the oddball was nowhere to be seen.

A little later on, Dawn went to the toilet, leaving the bedroom door ajar and Nancy sat with her back to the window, looking at the light from the landing shining into the room. She wished Dawn would hurry back because she was getting a little uneasy being on her own with that weirdo still on the loose. Then all of a sudden she detected that very same strong sweet aroma that had greeted her nostrils when she was in the back alleyway earlier, and her stomach lurched with fear. Something toppled the empty lemonade bottle off the window ledge, and it smashed on to the pavement below. Forcing herself to look, Nancy turned and saw a hand - a pale maroon coloured hand — reaching into the room to grab her. Before she could even cry out, Dawn came back into the room, and on seeing what was happening, she ran to the window and tried to slam it down hard on the groping arm but it vanished before she could trap it.

Nancy's hysterical screams after this latest trauma woke the whole household and ensured that she would never again be invited to a sleepover at Dawn's house. In fact, Dawn's father threatened that if he ever saw that girl on the premises again, he would physically throw her out on to the street by the scruff of her neck, which was a bit unfair, since it was his daughter's idea in the first place.

Nevertheless, the girls remained firm friends but they never did find out just who or what that stalker was, or why the police were chasing him that night. Perhaps someone had tipped them off after seeing him lurking on the backyard walls. Not knowing was the most difficult part and for years, they lived in mortal fear of encountering the uncanny stalker again, and Nancy, in particular, suffered harrowing nightmares about him until her premature death from a rare illness in 1974.

THE OUIJA

One humid afternoon in July 2005, forty-seven-year-old Jimmy from Toxteth turned the oven gas control to number 9, opened the oven door, and took out the shelves. He knelt down, put his head in the oven, and grimaced when he noticed the few spills of grease and fat from the exceedingly rare occasions when he and his flatmate had had the money to afford a roast. He swore vehemently at the world with all its unfairness, cruelty and sadness; he could not wait to get out of it. He wondered how long it would take before he was thoroughly gassed, and as the sweet, salty-smelling gas filled his nostrils, he thought about his flatmate 'Rella' (a vintage seventies slang-name for his best friend Joseph, who had always played truant around the 'Rella' - the railway cuttings in Edge Hill. It suddenly occurred to Jimmy that Rella might inadvertently kill himself by flicking on the light-switch if he came in after dark. The infinitesimal electric spark jumping between the contacts inside the light-switch cover could quite probably ignite the build up of natural gas in the flat and cause a massive explosion.

Jimmy thought it quite ironic that it was North Sea gas that would end his life. He remembered all of the hullaballoo when those fields of gas and oil had been discovered in the North Sea in the sixties, and by the early seventies everyone believed the hype on the television and in the newspapers - that the newly-discovered fields would mean cheaper gas in the home. The people of Britain were about to share in the new prosperity - but for him, like many others, the good times never arrived.

Jimmy's mind rambled on randomly in this way for some time, until he decided that suicide by gassing was taking too long (in fact, North Sea gas is not poisonous, like the old town gas used to be, but he did not know that) and so he grumpily withdrew his head from the oven and got to his feet - and then noticed that the gas control dial had been turned back to zero. He looked at the dial, puzzled, squinting in disbelief. He clearly recalled having turned it to full about ten long minutes ago.

He opened the barred kitchen window to let the gas escape, for gas there had certainly been - he could clearly smell it - then went into the living room and slouched down on the sofa. He opened his tobacco tin, took out a pinch of Golden Virginia and then pulled out a cigarette paper from its slim packet. A roll-up was created in seconds, and Jimmy instinctively reached for his lighter before realising at the last moment that lighting up would be a mistake, as he could still smell gas, even from the living room.

So he went out on to his front doorstep on Princes Road and lit up there, and half-way through the roll-up he saw the Rella riding towards him on his mountain bike. He carried the bike into the flat and swore as soon as he was over the threshold. "Ugh! What's that horrible smell?" he gasped. "There must be a gas leak!" and he turned to Jimmy with a shocked face. "Couldn't you smell it, Jim?"

"There isn't a leak - I erm - I left one of the gas rings on by mistake and forgot to light it."

"Well, you're getting careless in your old age. You could have blown us both to kingdom come."

They both went inside, but Jimmy carefully pinched the lit head of his roll-up first.

Ten minutes later the truth came out.

"You what? You tried to commit suicide? What for? Are you depressed again?" Rella was stunned and upset. "There's nothing worth topping yourself for," he told Jimmy, who had now switched on the television. He flipped through channels full of dreary repeats, cookery, DIY and gardening programmes that almost put him back in a suicidal frame of mind. "Tell me what goes on in there," said Rella, poking his middle finger at the crown of Jimmy's head - right on his bald spot, about which he was extremely touchy.

"Get off!" he cried, switching off the television and throwing the remote control against the wall. "It's okay for you, you've got college, and you're starting to snide off with your middle class mates and everything."

"Well, so what? Who's stopping you from going to college? I've tried to encourage you time and time again but you always say no one can teach you anything worth learning!" Rella retorted, and then he dwelt on the hurtful remark Jimmy had made about him "sniding off - slang for neglecting your old friend to form a friendship with a new mate. "I haven't snided off with anyone," Rella told him, as he removed his cycling helmet. "I'm forty-eight years of age, for god's sake, not a kid. I'm bound to make new acquaintances in a college class of like-minded people. It's not a sin, you know. You don't own me."

"Oh, it's not really that. I'm just sick of being skint!" said Jimmy, burying his face in his hands. He hated Rella seeing him cry but he couldn't stop himself. "There are people far worse off than you, Jimmy!" Rella reminded him. "People with mortgages to keep up with, and kids who demand clothes and shoes with the right logos on them. Anyway, you were on top of the world last week when you won a few bob on the horses - you can take the ups but you can't take the downs! That's your trouble, mate."

"Actually, I didn't win on the horses; I sold your laptop," Jimmy confessed, and now the tears were unstoppable.

This time Rella could not miss the tears, but his sympathy for his old friend was diametrically opposed to his loathing of his self pity and hopeless lifestyle, especially now he knew the truth about his laptop. At the time, Jimmy had claimed he had tackled a hooded youth with a knife who had sneaked in through a window and snatched the laptop. He had shown Rella a bandaged hand where he had been knifed by the raider. No wonder he couldn't be persuaded to go for a tetanus jab at the walk-in clinic. It all made sense now.

Rella just wanted to give Jimmy a good hiding and shake him out of his misery, but they were good mates and he couldn't bring himself to do it. In recent weeks his old friend had been sinking deeper and deeper into debt and despair and on top of all that his year-long relationship with his girlfriend had just ended. When he thought of it like that, he was not surprised by his low mental state.

"If you kicked my head in, you'd be doing me a big favour," gulped Jimmy through the tears, which gave him a child-like quality.

"You need some proper help, Jimmy," said Rella earnestly, and he came around the sofa and sat next to him. It was horrible watching his best friend cry. "Depression is an illness, just like any other, and it has to be treated."

There came no reply, only the sound of weeping.

That night, a black man known only as Brother John turned up at the flat at 8pm. Rella answered the door but John looked straight past him until Jimmy came down the hallway and invited him in. Jimmy escorted Brother John into the spare room as Rella silently mouthed, "Who's the hell's he?"

Jimmy would not say and he closed the door of the spare room in Rella's face. Two more people turned up minutes later, and Jimmy hurried to the door and cordially invited them in. One of these people was known to Rella; he was an immaculately dressed Nigerian who went by the name of Tobias Conrad. He had lived in the same street as Rella down in Highbury five years back, and Conrad had a strange reputation - he was rumoured to dabble in the Occult and hypnotism. The other person was a little bald man in his fifties who didn't seem to know Conrad, but appeared to have merely arrived at the flat by coincidence at the same time as he had.

Rella's curiosity was aroused and he had to find out what was going on. He called to Tobias Conrad as he was being escorted into the spare room, and his former neighbour flashed a toothy smile and raised his eyebrows in recognition. He acknowledged Rella with a thumbs up gesture but Jimmy looked impatiently at his watch and said something to him, and then he and the other man hurried through the doorway into the room.

Rella rushed forward, and before the door of the spare room was closed in his face for a second time, he saw something very odd. There was an upturned glass in the middle of the round table in the room, and circled about the glass were white squares of paper. Jimmy and his guests were obviously about to dabble with an impromptu ouija board session. Rella called Jimmy out to speak with him in the hallway, and demanded to know what was going on and why he had called the three visitors to the flat. Jimmy rolled his eyes in irritation, emitted a loud sigh and said, "We are going to try and contact my auntie who died a year ago and ask her some questions. Is that okay by you?"

"I think you should get a grip, Jimmy - you don't even sound like yourself anymore," a concerned-looking Rella told him. "I know exactly what you're planning to do in there. Do you know what those things can conjure up?"

"What things?" Jimmy asked, with a smug condescending expression on his face. "You're acting like you're my mum, or something. Get out of my face, will you? We were just about to start."

Rella stood his ground, naively thinking his friend would listen to him, "The ouija board - people have been possessed after using them; and not only that, I know for a fact that Tobias Conrad has done all sorts of dodgy and dangerous things using black magic and voodoo."

Jimmy was in no mood for argument and just shook his head and went into the room to proceed with the ouija session. A long suffering and frustrated Rella sighed and went into the living room, switched on the television and turned up its volume. His friendship with Jimmy was being tested to the limit.

Almost an hour later, Rella thought he heard screams coming from the spare room. He turned the sound down on the television and listened. Yes, there was no doubt about it. Rella belted out of the living room, crossed the hallway and burst into the spare room, which was lit only by a single candle in the middle of the circular table. The scene that greeted Rella's eyes in that dimly lit room still haunts him today. Jimmy, Brother John, Tobias Conrad, and the little bald man in his fifties, were all quivering with fright at the table, as they sat bolt upright in their chairs. The whites of their eyes were visible, because their eyeballs had rolled up into the backs of their heads, and their tongues wormed about like snakes in their open mouths. The wine glass that ouija board was lying on its side, rolling in a circle around its circular base, and the cut-out paper squares, upon which the letters of the alphabet and the numbers nought to nine had been written, were scattered all about the place.

Rella tried to 'wake' Jimmy by gently shaking him, but he did not react. Tobias Conrad then let out the most spine-chilling scream, and his mouth opened wider and wider, until suddenly a white globular object emerged. Rella later described the appearance of this object as "Some kind of bubble, smooth as a white snooker ball, and about the same size, or perhaps a bit bigger."

This white shiny sphere's surface began to ripple, and steadily increased in size as shapes began to develop upon its skin - and then it metamorphosed into a face - a grotesque, hideous-looking face which grinned evilly out at the little assembly, as Rella looked on in horror. He put his hands under Jimmy's armpits and physically dragged him from the table and out of the room, fearing that at any minute the shocking 'thing' would leap out of Conrad's mouth and attack them all.

Jimmy weighed seventeen stone and it was a formidable task to drag him into the living room, but the fear inside Rella boosted his strength, and he managed to haul his unconscious friend as far as the hearth rug and then turned and closed the living room door in a daze. He panted and looked around for something with which to revive Jimmy. He grabbed the bottle of brandy from the drinks cabinet in the corner, unscrewed its top and placed the mouth to his inert friend's lips. The bottle was carefully tilted, and Jimmy coughed and spluttered as he opened his eyes. He looked deeply confused, startled and scared.

Rella helped his disorientated friend on to the sofa and asked him what had happened. Jimmy then proceeded to reveal his pathetic plan; a wretched scheme that had its origins in pure greed, in getting something for nothing. "We tried to contact some sort of spirit - a demon or something. Toby Conrad said it just demanded one life, one soul, and it would answer any question about the past, present or future that we asked it."

"And I bet that question had something to do with making money!" Rella said through gritted teeth.

"We just wanted it to tell us next week's lottery numbers," Jimmy admitted, feeling foolish, and his tongue licked the remnants of brandy from his lips.

"You what?"

"The Euromillions lottery," Jimmy explained, and was about to go into all the details - how there had been a six-week roll-over and almost a hundred million pounds could be won, and how Toby Conrad had only charged him four hundred pounds for the ouija session, payable in four instalments.

Rella butted in, unable to contain himself any longer. "Wait there a minute!" he said, and bravely charged back into the spare room to find that Brother John had left. The unknown visitor — whom he later discovered was a homeless man called Robertson - was standing over Conrad, feeling his pulse. Rella watched him like a hawk, because the unconscious Nigerian was wearing an expensive Rolex watch. When Tobias Conrad came to his senses, he looked very poorly, and refused to say anything to Rella or Jimmy. He left the ground floor flat and hailed a cab on Princes Road, taking him to God knows where. Robertson left soon afterwards, and weeks later, Jimmy revealed the full extent of his shameful plan; that the homeless man's soul was to have been sacrificed to the demon, in exchange for the lottery numbers.

Rella thought the whole ouija business was utterly scandalous and could so easily have ended with fatal consequences. According to Jimmy, the glass on which the four men had rested their forefingers had slid about frantically, spelling out the first three numbers, but Brother John had then taken his finger off the glass after saying that he sensed the Devil in the room and he then began to recite the Lord's Prayer. It was at that point that Jimmy had passed out. Rella told him about the evil-looking 'head' that he had seen emerging from Conrad's mouth, but Jimmy thought his friend was simply trying to scare him out of ever playing with ouijas again. Rella proved to be a very good and loyal friend and eventually convinced Jimmy to attend college with him, and as a result of completing a course in e-commerce, Jimmy now runs an online business.

A few weeks after the ouija episode, forty-five-year-old Dolores McNamara won the Euromillions Lottery game and broke all records by netting seventy-seven million pounds. Jimmy immediately noticed that the first three winning numbers for that unprecedented win were the same as the first three numbers the ouija had spelt out. So maybe it had not been a trick, after all. He felt sick when he saw a photograph in the newspaper of Mrs McNamara holding the huge cheque, but Rella pointed out that winning such a large amount of money almost always had a downside to it. Jimmy disagreed and claimed he would sell his very soul to obtain that much wealth.

Not long afterwards, it was reported that Mrs McNamara, a mother of six, had not only become plagued by death threats and kidnap plots, but had also begun to receive sackloads of begging letters - fifteen thousand of them, to be exact.

"Is that what you want, Jimmy?" Rella's face popped over the top of the tabloid page on which the Lottery story was printed. "You'd sell your pathetic soul for that, eh?"

"Ah, the papers exaggerate everything. How could you not have a ball with that kind of money?"

Now this isn't the end of the story. Strange things happened in that abode on Princes Road which had, without a doubt, been evoked by the ouija board. One evening, Jimmy had just arrived home and inserted his key in the front door lock, when, before he could turn it, the door knocker rose and fell several times. Then a hand emerged from the letterbox flap and Jimmy thought it was just Rella messing about, but as the front door opened and swung inwards, the fingers of the hand were still protruding from the letterbox. Jimmy looked round the other side of the door and found that there was no one there. He looked back again at the front of the door and was taken aback to find that the two fingers of the inexplicable hand were not only still there, but were giving him the highly-offensive V-sign.

There was no way that Jimmy was going to go into the house after that and he ran away in fear down the road and ended up at a friend's house on High Park Street, where he stammered out a garbled account of the disembodied hand. His friend concluded that Jimmy must be on drugs to come up with such a stupid tale.

Three days later, Jimmy was watching a film on television in the living room, at around two in the morning, when his nostrils suddenly detected a truly horrible odour. He walked about the place sniffing the air, to try and detect the source of the smell and his nose led him into the hallway, where three bluebottles whizzed past him and flew into the living room. The foul stink was definitely becoming stronger, and as Jimmy walked back into the living room, he saw something that sent him running into Rella's bedroom.

On the sofa, there was an old woman, covered from head to foot in crawling, squirming maggots. Her eyes were closed and her mouth was open, and out of her mouth, a thin sprig of some plant protruded with leaves on. Bluebottles were buzzing around the stinking corpse in a frenzy of excitement. It was a scene straight from hell. Jimmy backed away and bumped into the doorframe of the living room in his panic to get away. He ran down the hallway and burst into Rella's bedroom to awaken him.

When the two men returned to the living room, the rotten corpse had vanished, but its stench still lingered, and Rella had to open the windows and front door of the flat in order to get rid of the repulsive smell that was making them both retch. Enough was enough, and within a week, Jimmy and Rella had moved to a flat over a shop on Bold Street.

I researched the history of the Princes Road address that Jimmy and Rella had been forced to abandon and discovered something of great relevance that turned Jimmy stone cold when I told him about it.

During the 1930s, an elderly man and his sister (they were both in their seventies) had lived at the address. The pair were very close and when the sister died from choking on her food, the brother refused to believe she was really dead. He failed to inform the authorities, or indeed anyone, about her death, and simply left her body to decompose in the front parlour of the house. Some six months later, the awful smell from the putrefying corpse seeped out through the walls and under the floorboards of the house and the neighbours became suspicious, as it had not gone unnoticed that the sister had not been seen for quite some time.

The police called at the house and had no difficulty in finding the old woman's corpse, which was lying in a divan in a very advanced state of decomposition. They also noticed something macabre and rather peculiar: a woody stem of about fourteen inches in length and sprouting leaves, was sticking out of the dead woman's mouth. During the post-mortem the coroner discovered that the deceased had eaten tomatoes just before she had choked, and one of the seeds from a tomato had lodged itself between one of her teeth and the fleshy gum. That seed had germinated in the damp fertile environment of the rotting gums and had flourished and grown into a stem in the six months the body had lain rotting.

The ghost of this unfortunate old lady was said to still haunt her house, though she was quite a friendly ghost, but sometimes a terrible smell would invade the front parlour, and when the ghost's former home was subdivided into flats, she would be seen all over the building, often switching on lights and meddling with electrical equipment at all times of the day and night. Perhaps it was her presence that had turned the gas off when Jimmy made his botched suicide attempt. The old woman's ghost is still said to be active today at the flats on Princes Road.

When the ouija board is used at a dwelling, it is imperative that a 'closure' ritual be performed at the end of the session, otherwise some of the trouble-making spirits which may have been unleashed, can start to frequent the location recurrently and usually cause havoc with the living. After a session, it is also vital to place the glass in an upright position and then to thank the spirits for cooperating with words such as, "Spirit, I thank you and bid you goodnight," which is how some seasoned practitioners of the ouija end these sessions. Others make the sign of the cross and recite the Lord's Prayer at the close of the session.

Most people think the ouija is only used by sensation-seekers, by people who have become disenchanted with their religion, and also by the just plain curious. In reality, the social spectrum of people using the 'speaking glass' and other methods of divination is much broader. I even know of company directors who have resorted to the ouija to see if they can determine the best days for floating their company's shares.

If you are intending to use the ouija, please take the matter very seriously and if you are religious, keep something that is representative of your faith - a crucifix, or a Bible perhaps - close at hand. At the end of the session -acknowledge the help of the spirit for the purposes of closure. However, if you are of a very nervous disposition my advice to you is not to dabble with the ouija, and if any of the people who intend to participate in the ouija session are showing any signs of anxiety, they must be asked to leave before the sitting commences.

PHANTOM ROAD

The M62 motorway, opened in stages between spring 1971 and 1976, is one hundred and seven miles long, and connects the cities of Liverpool and Hull via Manchester and Leeds, so joining the traditionally opposed counties of the red rose and the white rose. Accents change along this phenomenal trans-Pennine highway, which, at one point, reaches an altitude of one thousand two hundred and twenty-one feet on Windy Hill - making the great East-West motorway the highest in the UK. The M62 has also had its fair share of paranormal occurrences over the years. Here are just a few of these supernatural mysteries of the tar macadam to tantalise us.

In the early autumn of 1980, lorry drivers in the Manchester area threatened to boycott the Burtonwood motorway service station on the M62, near Warrington, because they were being charged ten pence for a pint of boiling water, which the drivers used to brew their own tea. A district official of the Transport and General Workers' Union, who represented the thousands of protesting lorry drivers, demanded free water on tap from the service station, so the drivers could use their own teabags to make their refreshments, instead of having to pay twenty-one pence for a mug of tea.

John Shuttlewood, an HGV driver in his forties, was travelling along the M62 in his vehicle one dark morning in October of that year, talking about the boiling water 'scandal' to his nineteen-year-old son Eddy (who often accompanied him on long runs to and from Manchester) when something quite bizarre took place. The lorry trundled through Junction 6 of the M62, and the motorway from that point on, when bound for Liverpool, curves to the right, but on this dark misty morning at 6.30am, the motorway somehow was veering to the left - in the direction of Netherley, and Childwall Golf Course - which, of course, was impossible.

The sun had not yet risen, and with only the artificial light of the highway's sodium lamps to show the way, Mr Shuttlewood did not doubt the 'phantom road' that stretched up ahead of him, but his son Eddy quickly woke his father from the 'open eye' dream. The teenager saw what was happening and seized the wheel and tried to turn it right, but his father wrestled it back to the left. The lorry was seconds away from disaster, when suddenly, Mr Shuttlewood realised his panicking son was right, and he swung the vehicle into a sharp curve to the right.

The ghostly road that had so nearly led to disaster faded away before the eyes of both father and son, and the real road reappeared. The lorry almost jack-knifed as it swerved dramatically under John Shuttlewood's sharp steering, and luckily he quickly regained control of the vehicle, even though he gave the drivers of other vehicles a nasty scare.

Fearing ridicule, and thinking it would affect his future employment prospects, John did not mention the motorway mirage to anyone for many years, until he wrote to me about this phantom road in 2006 and asked if I had heard about any similar experiences. I certainly had and I told him how a Mr Jacobs had seen something similar - a phantom carriageway - as he was travelling towards Liverpool down the M62 one evening in the summer of 2002. As forty-two-year-old Mr Jacobs passed under the Whitefield Lane flyover, he saw a carriageway, strangely devoid of any traffic, veering off to his left. He had never noticed this carriageway before, and assumed it had recently been created, because he had not used the motorway for a few years. He carried on driving along the original direction of the M62 and as he did so he glanced over at the new carriageway, and noticed that there were no cars on it and stranger still, the road ended in a large cloud of dark vapour, as if there had been a fire, or an accident over there.

Jacobs mentioned this new carriageway to a cousin in Childwall, and was told there was no such new road after the Whitefield Lane flyover. Jacobs insisted that there was and that he had seen it with his own eyes.

A fortnight later, Jacobs left his Salford home and visited his cousin in Childwall again. This time it was broad daylight, and as Jacobs passed under the Whitefield Lane flyover, he expected to see the carriageway that branched off to the left, but instead he saw only farmland stretching towards Childwall Golf Course. The stretch of carriageway he had seen two weeks before, which he estimated to be over a quarter of a mile in length, had now vanished without a trace.

In 2003, Jacobs was invited to a christening by a friend in Leeds named Les Groom, and after the ceremony, there was a party at Groom's house. One of the topics of conversation that arose amongst the men of the party was cars - who had the fastest model, the newest, or the most economical vehicle and so on. Then the subject turned to humorous incidents and experiences on the road, and Les Groom suddenly mentioned something that stunned Mr Jacobs. He said he had been driving along the M62 one morning at 4am, on his way to work, (this was in the late 1990s, when he lived in Manchester and worked at a factory in Liverpool). Just after he had passed under a bridge, Les had been surprised to see a new completed stretch of motorway that branched out from the M62 and headed towards the sewage works on Coney Lane. This lane is practically in the same area as the phantom road seen by John Shuttlewood and Mr Jacobs. Les Groom felt impelled to drive down the 'new' road, even though it would have taken him miles away from his destination, but he snapped out of the trance-like state at the last minute and managed to overcome the strange compulsion. If Les had obeyed the lure of the spectral motorway, God knows what would have happened, but at least we might have got some answers.

In April 2009, I received a letter from Peter Beresford, of Heswall, who told me of a further paranormal incident he had experienced in 1979, which dovetails neatly with the aforementioned accounts. This is what he wrote:

One summer Sunday morning around 5.30am I was

travelling to Liverpool along the M62 and at the stretch of that motorway between Junctions 1 and 5, I not only saw a misty carriageway leading off to the left towards farmland, I also felt strongly compelled to drive down it. Luckily, I resisted the strange impulse and carried on my way. I knew there was no carriageway leading from the M62 at the point where I saw one, but I consulted the maps of my AA atlas anyway, and saw that there was categorically no exit between Junctions 1 and 5. To this day I'm at a loss to explain what I witnessed. Did something try to make me crash that day by coaxing me down an illusionary carriageway?

A WARNING FROM BEYOND

It was a strange way to meet, yet a sweet one, nevertheless. A few years ago, Hayden, an insomniac in his forties, was sitting up in bed one morning just after three o'clock, reading a magazine he had kept from his youth called *Omni* - a now-defunct American publication, which featured articles on science fact, futurology and science fiction.

As Hayden lay engrossed, rereading the old magazine by the soft light of his bedside lamp, he thought he heard noises above: the dull sounds of clunking footsteps moving across the ceiling of his basement flat on Liverpool's Mount Street. The flat upstairs, on the ground floor, was vacant, yet there was no mistaking the sound, someone was definitely moving about up there. In retrospect, Hayden agrees that he should have called the police as soon as he heard the footsteps, but instead, he put on his trousers, coat and slippers, and grabbed an unlikely weapon - chosen because he could find nothing better in a hurry - a strong old golf umbrella.

He crept up the stairs from the basement to the gate that was set into the black railings at the front of the Georgian house, unfastened the combination bicycle lock from its chain, opened the squeaky gate, and walked slowly along the pavement until he was at the foot of the three steps leading up to the old front door of the building. There was a light on right at the far end of the hallway of the ground floor flat, and as Hayden watched, he briefly saw the shadowy movement of someone small, possibly a youth.

He went up the three front steps and was surprised an a little spooked to find that the front door was open by a few millimetres. Hayden gently pushed it open and was then able to get a better view of the fuzzy silhouette visible through the etched baroque designs of the vestibule door, which was patently the outline of a woman. He opened the vestibule door and a woman - about five-foot-three in height with a pale round face and shoulder-length golden auburn hair - stood there, with a look of equal surprise on her face. The two strangers looked at one another in silence for a few moments, until Hayden finally spoke, "Excuse me, but have you just moved in here? I'm sorry if you have, but I thought the flat was empty and that you might be a trespasser."

The woman gave no reply and instead reached into her handbag and withdrew a mobile phone. Although she was wary of Hayden's presence, she thought he looked and sounded quite urbane, and facially he reminded her of the late debonair actor William Franklyn (of the old "Schhh! You know who!" Schweppes tonic water television adverts).

"I live in the basement flat down below - down in the dungeons," Hayden laughed awkwardly. He realised that it could be construed that he posed a threat to this woman -whoever she was - and so he smiled as unthreateningly as he could, and backed away towards the front door.

The woman suddenly found her voice, "I used to live here," she said, rather dreamily, after somehow sensing that Hayden was a decent man who meant her no harm.

"I see." Hayden wasn't too sure exactly what her words meant, but he nodded and smiled anyway.

"My name's Hayden, by the way," he told her.

The woman approached, and her low heels made that distinctive clunking sound that had first alerted him to her presence. "My name's Dia - short for Lydia," she told him in a genial tone. At closer quarters he could see she was between about thirty-eight to forty-two years old, and rather good-looking.

Hayden nodded, "Pleased to meet you, Dia."

"Is it raining outside?" Dia asked, noting the golf brolly Hayden was carrying.

Hayden grinned sheepishly and explained its intended role. Luckily, Dia could appreciate the funny side of it all.

In fact Dia trusted Hayden enough to go down to his flat and have a cup of tea with him. She was offered a sherry but declined, as she would have to drive home soon, she said. She sat on Hayden's wine-coloured buttoned leather sofa as she told him how she was "a hopelessly incurable nostalgic" who liked to visit her old childhood home every now and then, for old time's sake.

"Hmm, I wonder why I've never heard you before then?" Hayden mused.

"I usually wear flat shoes, but I forgot and came in my heels tonight. Don't know why, my feet are killing me." Dia scanned the bookshelf, which covered the whole of one wall and was stacked with tomes on the paranormal. She realised she was in the basement of her old home, the place that truly scared her, and now that place was someone else's flat and was barely recognisable. It was so sad seeing the house divided into flats like this. Father should never have sold the place, Dia thought.

"How did you manage to get in upstairs? Have you got a skeleton key?"

"Stroke of amazing luck, actually," Dia replied. "A few years ago I was sitting outside the place in my car, reminiscing as usual, when an estate agent was accompanying a couple who were viewing the flat. He dropped the key as he was talking to them, and neither he nor the couple noticed. There was a heavy thunderstorm going on at the time, mind you, so that's probably why. The estate agent hurried on down the pavement, quickly pointing to another flat with a To Let sign outside. He was obviously keen to get out of the rain as soon as possible and so I just left the car and went and picked up the key and pocketed it. As I was about to drive off, I saw the estate agent coming back, looking worried. He was looking down at the ground as he walked back towards the door of the flat, obviously looking for the lost key. I quickly drove off and returned a few days later. I wondered if he had perhaps had the locks changed, as the address was written on the cardboard tag of the key he had dropped, but luckily he hadn't."

"You could get into trouble for doing that, you know," Hayden warned her with a warm smile. "Why don't you just buy or rent the place, if you love it so much? Are you married?"

"No, divorced, five years. I can't afford to rent or

buy at the moment, and I'm not sure if it's a good thing to try and go back and live in a place that has so many memories. They say you should never look back."

"My old house was demolished years ago in Bristol. If it was still standing, I'd move heaven and earth to get the money to buy it." Hayden's eyes turned pensively to stare into space, to bygone, better times.

"So, I can see that you're a bit of a nostalgic too," Dia smiled wryly. She looked at the clock. It was half-past three in the morning, time she was going. "Gosh! Look at the time! I'd better let you get some sleep, or you'll be shattered in the morning."

"No, I'm fine, I'll be up till seven at least."

Hayden was really enjoying this woman's company and didn't want the night to end.

"What about work?" asked Dia, placing the cup of tea and its saucer on the coffee table and getting up from the sofa.

"Oh, I'm between jobs at the moment, and to be honest, the rest is doing me good." Hayden got up from the armchair and set down the mug of tea on the mantelpiece. "I'm divorced too, as it happens. Have been for nearly ten years. I used to publish poetry, but there's no money in it anymore."

"Well, Hayden, it's been great having this little chat with you in the wee small hours-"

Dia just stood there with some awkwardness after she had said this, as if she wanted to add something else, but didn't dare.

"Maybe -" Hayden started.

But in the same briefest moment, Dia said, "Perhaps -"

"Sorry -" Hayden apologised, and nodded to her nervously, "you first."

"Oh, I was just going to say, if you like, we could have another chat like this over a coffee sometime?" Dia suggested, and blushed slightly.

"Yes. of course," said Hayden, trying not to appear too eager. "That would be lovely."

Dia and Hayden started dating, and it soon became apparent that they were made for each other. They loved the same things, which included everything to do with the Victorian age and the supernatural. It wasn't long before they decided to live together, and they moved into Hayden's flat - which felt so familiar to Dia, of course, because it had once been the basement of her childhood home. As a hobby Hayden and Dia began to investigate reports of ghosts and alleged local hauntings in the Northwest and beyond. Dia even placed an ad in the local newspaper which read:

Is your home haunted?
Have you seen a ghost? Serious investigators of the paranormal are looking for ghosts to investigate.
Telephone 0151 280 XXXX
or Email: haydendia@yahoo.co.uk

A copy of the same ad was also placed on the noticeboard in the local supermarket amongst all the wanted and for sale items. Two days later, there was a telephone call from an elderly woman who had an unusual story to tell. Hayden picked up the phone, and after discovering that the caller - a woman named Mrs Greer - was calling in response to the ghost advertisement, he motioned for Dia to listen in on the extension.

Mrs Greer began by telling them that her twenty-year-old grand-daughter Sophie worked in a fish and chip shop in Anfield, and on several occasions over the last three weeks, always at night, a terrifying apparition had been coming into her place of work - a man with a disfigured face. What was more, this uncanny entity had even followed Sophie home after the chippie had closed, and she had almost been knocked down by a taxi as she tried to shake off the eerie stalker. Other people had seen the ghost, including customers and staff at the chippie.

Mrs Greer wanted to know if Hayden could lay the ghost to rest, exorcise it, or whatever the ritual was to rid Sophie of this paranormal persecutor. Hayden felt sorry for the girl and equally could not wait to get his hands on a real case at last, so he promised he would give it his best shot, and he and Dia embarked on their first proper ghost busting case.

They began their investigations by visiting Sophie at her home during the day and writing down her description of the ghost in great detail. She was visibly shaking as she recalled the phantom's face, which looked as if it had melted and the hair on its head looked singed. It always wore a green long-sleeved shirt emblazoned with the Carlsberg logo right across it, and black shorts and green socks. Sophie was even able to state that the solid-looking spectre wore black trainers. This seemed a pretty surreal description, but it later made sense in the light of new information.

The figure had turned up at the fish and chip shop four times in all, and on one occasion it had made its appearance in the road where Sophie lived. Throughout the interview with her, Hayden and Dia could plainly see that the girl had been truly terrified by something outside of her everyday experiences.

The investigative duo spent the first evening sitting in Dia's parked car close to the chippie, keeping a watch out for the alleged ghost. But that first evening was notable only for the passing of a gang of noisy youths, who pounded their fists on the roof of the car, and the unwanted attention of a policeman on the beat, who asked Hayden and Dia what they were doing there and who they were waiting for.

On the second night, Hayden and Dia were given permission by the Taiwanese owner of the eatery to wait in the room adjacent to the chippie's kitchen, which gave access through a doorway to the counter where Sophie was serving the customers. In the other room the owner of the establishment was watching television. At 11.20pm that night, there was a strange yelping sound, which startled Hayden as he was reading a book to kill time. Dia was sitting near to him, sipping a soft drink, and her large eyes widened as she exchanged glances him. They both jumped to their feet and hurried through the doorway. Sophie was slowly inching backwards towards them, and they saw a young man in a green top and black shorts standing in the shop doorway. It was raining heavily outside and there were no customers about.

Sophie turned to Hayden and cried, "That's him!" before diving into the back room. Hayden and Dia had plenty of time to study the grotesque figure as it stood stock-still in the doorway of the chippie, as though it had been planted there. Its face was even more horrifically misshapen than either of them had ever imagined; like some wax head from Madame Tussauds that had been left in the oven for half an hour. Livid patches of red raw exposed flesh stood out prominently from the sooty, partly melted face. As Sophie had described so accurately, the ghost wore a 2004 Liverpool FC grass-green goal-keeper kit.

The amateur investigators were so horrified by the ghoulish spectacle of the melted face that they forgot to collect any evidence with their digital cameras. After a while, the figure turned away without a word and walked off into the rainy night. As Dia tried to lift the counter flap to go after the ghost, Hayden athletically slapped his palms down flat on the counter top, then leapt straight over it and dashed out into the street. The rain was coming down in torrents by this time and Hayden was soon drenched to the skin. The figure was becoming transparent as he watched it, and although its leg movements suddenly ceased, it continued to glide across the road and between two parked cars at the other side.

Hayden looked back and saw Dia emerge from the chippie. He pointed at the retreating ghost and then rushed across the road in pursuit of it, dodging a beeping hackney cab as he did so. Dia eventually caught up with Hayden and the two of them followed Sophie's spectral stalker, each stopping momentarily to take pictures with their cameras.

On Priory Road, a group of girls hurrying along in the rain passed within feet of the semi-transparent figure, and yet were completely oblivious to it. Then the ghost darted through a wall - straight into Anfield Cemetery. At this point an icy wind, of almost gale force, buffeted Dia and Hayden, and this, together with the pelting rain, forced them to give up the chase for the night. There was no way they were prepared to go chasing into a graveyard in such horrendous conditions. They returned to the fish and chip shop and tried to console Sophie, but the girl was totally distraught and said she felt victimised. Why her? and when was it all going to end, she wanted to know. Hayden and Dia took her home and for almost an hour they sat with her and her mother, who was just as worried about the strange visitations, especially as her husband was currently working nights at a factory in Knowsley.

"Why does it keep haunting me? What have I done wrong?" Sophie kept on asking Hayden, as if he could provide an answer, just like that. "I'm not sure, but in these types of cases there often turns out to be an obvious reason," Hayden told her, and sipped a mug of strong sugarless tea - just the way he liked it. "Have any close friends or boyfriends of yours died in the past few years?"

"No, why?" Sophie replied, looking at the preoccupied ashen face of her mum, sitting next to her on the sofa.

"Specifically, do you perhaps recall anyone you knew in the past dying in a fire?" Hayden asked the girl.

Sophie thought about the unusual question for a while, then a look of slow realisation could be seen in her eyes. She turned to her mother and said, "Of course! That lad - Craig. Do you remember?"

"Oh, God, yes! How could I forget? He was so creepy."

Sophie's mum then told Hayden and Dia about a

nineteen-year-old boy named Craig, who had developed a crush on Sophie three years ago. It had all started when he sent her a Valentine card. She didn't fancy the lad in the least, and so she did not return him any affection, but he began to stalk her in person and even bombarded her with text messages, which bordered on the abusive in the end. Sophie's father ended up going to have words with Craig's dad about his son's unacceptable behaviour. Craig was thrashed by his father and the police were called in when neighbours heard the lad's screams.

Craig left home one night soon afterwards and travelled with a friend to a camp site in Wales. One night he and his friend built a camp fire and sat around it swigging back bottles of cheap cider. Craig's friend eventually fell asleep in a drunken state, and tragedy struck some time afterwards. It seems that Craig, in a highly intoxicated state, had choked on his own vomit and had then fallen to the ground unconscious - face down in the fire!

"Was Craig buried in Anfield Cemetery, by any chance?" Dia asked, holding her breath.

Sophie nodded, "Yes - yes he was. Oh, my God! Do you think it's *his* ghost?"

Memories of that awful time came flooding back and the girl squeezed her mother's hand.

"Well, it's a possibility," Dia replied, but decided not to upset the mother and daughter any further by drawing attention again to the gory details of the ghost's melted face and the red raw flesh.

To Sophie, Dia said, "If anything happens - anything at all - even if its four o'clock in the morning, please call us - okay?"

The girl nodded.

"Thanks," said her mother.

As soon as Hayden and Dia were home they downloaded the photographs from their cameras into the computer and saw, just as they had expected, nothing but a cluster of mundane orbs (caused by the reflection of the camera flash on the mid-air raindrops) and a faint blue smudge - the only visible trace of the actual ghost. Even the smudge was almost impossible to analyse, because the camera shake in the shots was too prominent. When the CCTV footage of the chippie was examined the following afternoon, the doorway was found to be tantalisingly out of shot, so there was no sign of the ghost on the tape either.

Sophie's grandmother, Barbara, then had a word with Craig's grandmother and gleaned the plot number of the grave where the young man had been buried. Barbara passed this potentially valuable information on to Hayden and Dia, as they had told Sophie and her mother that they would be prepared to hold a vigil in Anfield Cemetery, even though it was illegal to do so.

Around this time, Sophie's nerves had become so taut, that she and Rob, her boyfriend of three weeks, decided to take a five-day holiday in the Lake District. Sophie also decided to hand in her notice at the fish and chip shop, and the owner of the business said he was sorry to see her leave, as she had always been a very punctual and efficient worker.

Over three nights that week, Hayden and Dia, wrapped up in heavy winter clothing, and having armed themselves with all sorts of reputed 'ghost repellents', including crosses made of rowan, bound with red string, and of course two copies of the Holy

Bible, bravely roamed the graveyard close to the final resting place of Craig.

On the third night, an unexpected fog from Liverpool Bay invaded the city. The one hundred and ten acres of the cemetery were already in darkness, with the faintest of illumination from the sodium lamp-posts bleeding into the fringes of the necropolis, but the fog turned the whole graveyard into a vaporous limbo of impenetrable blackness. Hayden's torch was dying, but its weak orange beam suddenly caught movement, and for a moment he thought it was Dia, but she was just behind him. He called to her and she turned, sweeping her strong white flashlight beam - and the bright ray revealed something green moving about in the fog, about twenty yards ahead - and it was coming their way. The combined beams from the two flashlights both fell upon the distinctive green LFC goalkeeper kit. The beams then crept ever so slowly upwards and revealed once more that horrifically burnt face and melted flesh. Craig, an amateur goalie at college and a loyal fan of the Reds, had been buried in that goalkeeper's home kit.

Hayden held out the Bible, but clumsily fumbled with the cross of rowan wood and then dropped it as he handed the torch to Dia. Dia felt more sympathetic towards the ghost than frightened or angry, and unbelievable as it seems, she looked upon the visitant from beyond the grave in a motherly way. This might have been her son, was the way she described it.

"In the name of Jesus Christ I command you to return to your grave!"

Keeping a firm voice, Hayden shouted at the ghost with the Bible thrust out before him, though it was difficult for him to keep his hand steady.

The ghost slowed but it did not stop and it was still headed towards the occult-dabbling duo.

Dia suddenly stepped out in front of Hayden and shouted, "Craig, we know you loved Sophie! We acknowledge that you loved her! What do you want?"

The ghost stopped in its tracks and a strange thing took place. The melted and charred face of the revenant swirled about as if it were made of liquid, and slowly reformed into the pale handsome face of a young man with a very sad pair of dark eyes. This was obviously the face of Craig before he had become so terribly disfigured. Yet his lips moved in an odd manner, and didn't seem to be synchronised with the words that were uttered. "I had to come back to warn Sophie (and he gave her surname too), because she is seeing a man named Rob. He is an evil man, who will kill her if she stays with him."

Hayden and Dia were speechless. The ghost had their full and undivided attention.

"I won't be able to come back again, so please warn Sophie for me," Craig's ghost said, its voice becoming notably weaker with each spoken word.

"Don't worry, Craig, we will tell her, and may you now rest in peace," promised Dia, solemnly.

The mist obscured the ghost for an instant, during which brief interval it must have vanished back into that undiscovered realm, for it was no longer anywhere to be seen. Hayden and Dia left the cemetery and quickly headed towards Sophie's home, even though it was 11pm. When they told the girl's mother about the warning, she visibly shuddered and goosebumps rose up on her arms and she suddenly confessed that she had never liked her daughter's boyfriend from the moment she had first set eyes on him. He struck her as a sly, conniving man, a bit too advanced for his twenty-five years for her liking.

Sophie's mother and father became so worried about the ghostly warning, that they decided to go and fetch their daughter back from the Lake District. When they arrived at the cottage in the Borrowdale valley, Sophie was perplexed, and her parents had to pretend that Angie, Sophie's favourite auntie, had fallen seriously ill, just to get her to come home. This tactic caused Rob to show his true colours and he came out with a string of swear words and shouted at Sophie's parents, saying they had ruined their holiday break. This sudden change in behaviour came as a complete shock to Sophie, who had never seen this aggressive side of her boyfriend, but then, she had only known him for less than a month.

There and then, Sophie's mother shepherded her daughter into the family car and told her everything that had happened in Anfield Cemetery. Sophie went white with shock. She went back inside the cottage and packed her belongings, with her father keeping closely by her side the whole time and then the family returned home. Rob stormed back into the cottage as they departed, shouting after them that the relationship was over.

After that, the ghost of Craig was seen no more, although Sophie, who, of course, now had a much kindlier view of her former boyfriend, visited his grave and laid some flowers and a thank-you card on it. It might have been just her imagination, but Sophie could have sworn she had felt the softest kiss on her lips as she knelt at the graveside.

By a coincidence, Craig's grandmother was visiting her grandson's grave at the same time, and she was puzzled by the thank-you card and floral tribute, so Sophie told her about the haunting. The old woman said she believed her because she had heard the same story from Sophie's Gran, Barbara. It was Craig's grandmother who explained to her why her grandson had been seen in the green shirt and black shorts; they were the clothes he had been buried in. Five months after this strange saga, Sophie learnt that Rob, her ex-boyfriend, had almost broken the jaw of his new girlfriend when he punched her because she refused to lend him money to go out with his mates.

As far as I know, Hayden and Dia are still investigating hauntings wherever they crop up. Perhaps you too could take a leaf out their book, if you dare, and become an investigator of the paranormal yourself. It is definitely more fun with a partner or a friend, so perhaps *you* could even form a ghost-hunters' club?

BUYER BEWARE

We all love a second-hand bargain, whether it is from Christie's, eBay, or the local Oxfam shop, but buyer beware, because some previously-owned items may have a secret supernatural history that you never bargained for.

A few years ago, sixty-seven-year-old Audrey, from Anfield, was browsing in a second-hand shop in Liverpool city centre when she spotted a cute framed print of a blonde blue-eyed cherubic-faced girl of about seven years of age. The girl wore a sad, haunted expression, with a single teardrop in the corner of her eye, and Audrey willingly paid the two pounds for the picture. Audrey's son mounted the print over the mantelpiece that same afternoon, and at teatime, Audrey's cousin Mona paid her a visit. When she saw the picture of the 'crying girl' on the wall she threw her hands up to her face and shrieked, "Take it down, Audrey! Throw it away!" When Mona had calmed down, she told Audrey that she had once owned the same picture of 'that thing' (as she called the unknown child) and it had brought nothing but bad luck and a series of deaths of those close to her. Audrey took her cousin's claims seriously, and immediately went outside to throw the picture in her blue recycling wheelie bin. As she was doing this, Audrey's next-door neighbour, an old disabled man named Billy, said, "Hey, if you're throwing that out, I'll have it, it's a nice picture, that."

"Oh no, Billy, you don't want it - it's unlucky," Audrey warned him, but Billy just smiled as he listened to his neighbour's superstitious cautionary tale, and he took the picture into his house, very pleased with his acquisition. On the following morning, the home help who visited Billy twice a day called at his home and found the front door lying wide open. Billy was dead in his armchair, though in death he was still staring in horror at the picture he had retrieved from Audrey's bin, which he had mounted on the wall near the window. The home help, Irene, recognised the unlucky picture at once. She later told Audrey the print was known as 'Sad Sarah', and she herself had once possessed a print of it, until she had had a long run of bad luck.

It was found that Billy had died of a massive heart attack, but Audrey firmly believed that the picture was somehow responsible for his early death. It could have all been down to coincidence, of course, but fortuity cannot explain the following strange incident, which stems, once again, from an item purchased in a second-hand shop.

In 1969, a young mother named Anne was living in Wavertree Gardens, a tenement overlooking

Wavertree Playground and the Wavertree High Street. Anne had recently lost her husband, and was struggling to cope financially to raise her nine-year-old son Harry and seven-year-old daughter Carol. Anne had a well-off sister named Wendy, who always visited at Easter time, along with her children who were always dressed up to the nines in the latest trendy gear. Not wanting her children to look shabby by comparison, Anne bought a child's smart-looking velvet suit and a little girl's frilly dress from a second-hand shop on Smithdown Road for her own children.

On Easter Sunday, at around 7pm, Harry left his home in the tenement block, kitted out in his 'new' suit and went to kick a ball around in Wavertree Playground. His mother watched him out of the window, and when it was getting towards dusk, she noticed a boy in what looked like pale clothes playing with him in the park. She shouted Harry in from the open window and asked him who the boy was.

"What boy, Mam?" Harry shouted back, after glancing about him, mystified.

"Him - there," said Anne and pointed to the pallid figure standing just to his right.

Harry looked around once more then shrugged in bafflement. As Harry came closer to his mother, so did the unknown boy, and Anne gasped was shocked, because she could now see that he was only wearing a pair of shorts and his body was chalk-white. Harry still couldn't see him, and soon he had vanished before Anne's eyes.

Anne never said anything more to Harry about the ghost that had followed him around Wavertree Playground, but she had a strong suspicion that the haunting had something to do with the second-hand velvet suit, and so she packed it up in an old suitcase, along with a set of rosary beads. Not sure what to do with it, she then put away in a wardrobe in the spare bedroom.

At half-past two that morning, Anne was awakened by a noise. She tried to open her eyes but the left one remained closed, its eyelid stuck by sleep. She squeezed both eyes shut again and opened them. The bedroom door handle was turning and the door was steadily opening and then Harry burst in with his unruly hair sticking up on end. His sleepy little sister Carol followed him, whimpering.

"Harry? Carol? What are you two doing up at this hour?" Anne asked, sitting up in bed.

"There's some lad in my room," Harry told his mother. "He pulled the blankets off me and he pulled our Carol's hair as well."

Anne was confused by Harry's words at first, and thought that perhaps he and his little sister had been messing around, having their usual pillow fights and such like, but then she realised the time and remembered the ghostly boy she had seen earlier in the evening. She told the children to stay in her room while she went off to investigate. She turned on the hallway light and listened - just the faint crying of Carol in her bedroom. She went into Harry's room and noticed that the place was a mess, not the usual kind of mess though - the blankets were strewn everywhere and so were the pillows.

Anne next went to the door of the spare room, where the velvet suit was packed away in the suitcase. She hesitated at the threshold of the room and listened again - no sound at all. So she turned the door handle, walked in and switched on the light. Everything was in its place - except for the wardrobe door, which was standing ajar. She walked slowly towards the wardrobe with the hairs on the nape of her neck bristling - then she heard the eerie, uncanny sniggering of a child, and it was coming from that wardrobe. Anne performed a u-turn and walked straight back out of the spare room, closing the door firmly behind her. She returned to her bedroom, put an upright chair against the door-handle and then told the children to get into her bed. The three of them lay huddled together, listening to the sounds of furniture and other objects being knocked over and thrown around in the other rooms. At one point, little Carol became hysterical, and when her mother managed to calm her down, she told her that a hand had come from under her pillow and its fingers had pulled her hair and pinched her nose till it hurt. Whether the child had dreamt this is still unknown.

Harry woke up again at around 7 o'clock and said that he had felt the mattress "go in" at the end of his mother's bed, as if someone was sitting there. When morning broke and the sun came shining into the room, it chased away all the fears of the traumatic night. Anne quizzed her son and daughter about the "boy" who had scared them last night, and both described a lad with blonde hair who only wore a pair of underpants. "His eyes looked horrible, Mum," Harry told her.

Anne went to tell a neighbour she had known for years about the ghostly goings-on, and the two women went together into the spare room to find the wardrobe tipped over on its side. When they righted it was found that its mirror was cracked right down the middle. Inside the overturned wardrobe, the suitcase containing the velvet suit was lying open. It was still inside but the rosary beads were found on the other side of the room.

Anne took the velvet suit back to the second-hand shop and demanded a full refund. The proprietor looked rather sly and seemed to know something about the suit that he was not prepared to reveal, but he just gave her the refund without saying a word.

Months later, Anne was chatting to an old friend who lived on Webster Road, off Smithdown Road, and discovered that she was well acquainted with the owner of the second-hand shop and she told her a shameful secret. The velvet suit had been unscrupulously removed from the body of a local boy who had died in a car crash a few years previously and sold on to the shop. The boy was supposed to have been buried in the suit in Toxteth Park cemetery - which was pretty close to the second-hand shop. After that suit was returned to the shop, the blonde boy was never seen again by either Anne, or her children.

GHOSTLY REPLAYS

If you look at a bright point of light, then quickly look away, you will often be aware of a fainter image of that light wherever you look for a short duration. What you are actually seeing is the imprint of the original light on the retina at the back of your eyeball - an everyday example of an after-image. Similarly, where a violent death has occurred, the sudden demise often leaves what seems to be another sort of 'after-image' on the very fabric of space-time. The same seems to be true of sound, and indeed of emotions too, and the following strange accounts illustrates this still largely unexplained phenomenon.

In 2002, an elderly woman contacted me to ask if I had ever heard of the phantom gunshots in the ground of Croxteth Hall. I had not at the time, but I mentioned the shots when I was a guest on Radio Merseyside's Billy Butler Show one afternoon and the station was inundated with calls from a significant fraction of the million-plus listeners. Over thirty callers claimed that they had heard what most described as a volley of shots within the grounds of the hall, and every witness said they had been heard at night. As I delved deeper into the incidents, another piece of information came my way, which seemed to make complete sense of the ballistic mystery.

Around the time of the infamous May Blitz of the Second World War, a man who worked as the boiler-man at Croxteth Hall was returning from fire-watch duty one night in the hall grounds, and as usual, his inquisitive young son was trotting alongside him. As father and son passed through the towering ancestral oaks and sycamores surrounding the Earl of Sefton's stately home, there was a faint rustle in the upper reaches of a large oak. The son heard it, and whispered to his father that someone was hiding in the topmost branches of the oak. The boiler-man quickly passed the information on to the soldiers who were stationed at Croxteth Hall, and within a few dramatic minutes, an officer was ordering his troops to form a circle around the base of the oak tree.

Rifles were raised and trained in the direction of the suspicious tree-dweller, and the officer issued three loud warnings for the person to show himself or herself and climb down immediately, or they would be shot. There was no reply. The officer then issued the grim order to fire and the rifles let loose a tremendous volley of bullets. A body plummeted through the tree, bouncing from branch to branch until it reached the ground with a sickening thud. A flashlight came tumbling after, still lit and one of the soldiers ran to extinguish it.

There was a communal gasp when the bloody corpse was rolled over and found to be wearing a British Army uniform. It transpired that the dead man had been a Belgian citizen, who had fled his Nazi-occupied homeland for England, and had subsequently enlisted in the British Army. However, it turned out that the soldiers had been right to shoot, because this individual was in fact a Nazi spy, who had been caught in the act of signalling to incoming German bomber planes with his torch from the treetop, alerting them to the fact that there were troops camped at nearby Croxteth Hall. Maybe it was that lethal hail of bullets, fired upon that Nazi collaborator all those years ago, that is still echoing down to our time.

In May 1985, there was another unsettling replay from the past, when two eleven-year-old Kirkby children came across a trail of blood mysteriously materialising on the ground behind a row of shops. The children ran home to their parents to tell them what they had seen, but when the adults went to inspect the blood, they found nothing there. Earlier that same morning, dozens of people had been startled by a semi-transparent woman, whom they immediately took to be a ghost, treading silently along the pavement of Kirkby's Stanton Crescent. As the ghost reached the end of the crescent it faded away.

Older residents shuddered when they heard of the ghostly woman and the phantom blood, because exactly seventeen years before on that very day - Friday, 10 May 1968 - an appalling incident had taken place in Kirkby, when thirty-eight-year-old Muriel White, a collector from Majestic Supply of London Road, went missing. Muriel had arranged to go for lunch at her mother's house on Denver Road, Kirkby, at 12.30pm that day, but the lunch went cold as her mother waited and waited for her daughter who would never arrive.

On the following day, at 10am, three boys made an horrific discovery: the upper part of a female body hidden under a sheet on waste ground off Stanton

Crescent. A few minutes later, the lower limbs of the unknown victim were found in bin lockers behind shops on James Holt Avenue, just two hundred yards away. The body parts were found to be the remains of missing collector Muriel White. She had been strangled before being dismembered. A local man was later arrested for the crime, and subsequently found guilty of manslaughter. All files relating to this horrific case - held under lock and key in the National Archives - are closed to public inspection until 2064.

The Kirkby paranormal incident is a prime example of what is known as an 'anniversary haunting' in the world of the supernatural. In such hauntings the ghost (or its bygone environment) puts in an appearance on the anniversary of some significant date - perhaps the anniversary of the ghost's death, or some other important event, usually connected to fatal consequences for the visitant.

Similar to the anniversary ghost is the 'seasonal apparition' - in which the manifested spirit tends to haunt a particular place at a specific time of the year. An example that comes to mind is the Swanside ghost, which, as its name suggests, habitually haunts a particular dwelling in the Swanside area.

In the autumn of 1967, twenty-two-year-old John Hollingworth, who was unemployed at the time, gambled and lost what little money he had at a card game at the Flying Saucer pub (now unimaginatively renamed the Mill House), on Alder Wood Road, Speke. When the towels were put on, at around 11pm, John faced a grim eight-mile odyssey on foot, all the way to his mother's home on Townsend Lane, in the Cabbage Hall area, and to make matters worse, a damp seaborne fog was steadily creeping its way across the Northwest.

The penniless young man pulled up the collar of his black jacket, put on his royal blue woollen hat, and walked out, head bowed, to face the cold night vapours. Minutes later, as he was passing the Dista factory on deserted Woodend Lane, the fog suddenly became even more opaque and an eerie silence enveloped the night traveller. It was as if the dense swirling mists had extinguished time itself and John felt more isolated than he had ever felt in his life. Suddenly, there came the sound of an approaching car and the diffused beams of light from its headlamps sliced through the fog. John Hollingworth was something of a car buff, and although he could only see the faint silhouette of the car as it slowed in its passing, he instantly recognised the distinctive shape of a 1940s Rover P2 Sports Saloon. The car rumbled to a halt about six feet ahead of him, and as he came up alongside it, the driver's face leaned towards the passenger window and tapped on it.

An old man's face was peering out at him with a concerned look and he beckoned John towards the vehicle with his hand. John went over to the old but very stylish-looking black car, and the passenger door clicked and opened slightly. He could now see that the driver was about seventy, with a good head of white hair, swept back and slicked. An atmosphere of Brylcreem and pipe tobacco hung in the air in the interior of the vehicle, evoking bygone days.

"Do you want a lift, laddy? That fog's bad for your chest," said the elderly driver.

"I'm on my way home," John told him. He smiled

nonchalantly, as if to show that he was impervious to the cold, but he could not prevent his teeth from chattering in the glacial marrow-chilling fog.

"Where's home?" asked the driver.

"The Cabbage Hall area."

The old man nodded, but told him he was only going as far as Swanside, which was not far from Knotty Ash, but the young penniless man was grateful for being taken that far in such inclement weather, and quickly put all his foolish pride aside and climbed into the quaint Rover.

The old man spoke not a word throughout the entire journey, and whenever John attempted to make pleasant conversation, not a syllable came back by way of reply. Instead, the old man just hummed some unidentifiable melody to himself the whole time. The fog, meanwhile, seemed to be condensing even further until it was almost black, and the streetlamps were gradually swallowed up by the gathering impenetrable gloom. Yet the old man continued to plough on into it at well over thirty miles per hour - a suicidal speed with such appalling visibility - but somehow he seemed to know, or sense, where he and his car were at any given moment, reading the bends and contours of the unseen road ahead, and anticipating sharp corners and obstacles with impeccable timing.

At last, the driver pulled up outside a just discernible quaint-looking cottage, not far from a railway line, John noted (presumably the one running between Broadgreen and Roby). John Hollingworth thanked him for the lift, opened the door and braced himself against the cold as he stepped out into the blurred Cimmerian fogbound street, unaware of where he was, or in which direction his home lay. The old man seemed to take pity on John, and invited him into the cottage for a whisky before embarking on the gruelling journey home — an invitation that was too tempting to refuse, despite his host's taciturnity.

John noted a dark-green wooden plaque on the cottage gate as he followed the man into the house, and it bore the name, 'Cranleigh' inscribed in gold letters. A friendly black and tan dog greeted John and the elderly man in the hallway of the cosy low-ceilinged cottage. "This is Billy," said the man, patting the dog on the head as it sniffed John's shoes. "He's very friendly." It was only at this juncture that the man finally introduced himself as Cyril Caddy and John shook his hand and gave him his name.

The living room was richly furnished with thick-piled Axminster carpets, George III mahogany chairs, and in the corner, to the right of the window, there was an item which John Hollingworth regarded with an envious eye - an elaborate black oak bureau. John had a long-held, secret ambition to become a writer, and had always fantasised about penning his first novel at just such a bureau.

The top of the bureau lay open and John admired the feathered quill pen resting in the inkwell, the bundles of important looking documents neatly bound with scarlet ribbons in their pigeon holes, the intriguing compartments filled with quality stationery, stamps, sealing wax, small box-files, and a huge magnifying glass with an ivory handle. After inviting John to take a seat, Mr Caddy then knelt on the hearth rug, struck a match, and lit several screwed up newspaper tapers that were inserted in the coal and sticks of wood that someone had previously laid in the grate.

John slowly began to relax and feel more comfortable and he took off his woollen hat and placed it on the left arm of the fireside leather armchair. As the kindling burst into flame, the old walnut grandfather clock in the corner started chiming midnight. The coals seemed to ignite spontaneously, giving off so much welcome warmth. John Hollingworth was not used to such comfort and luxury and he savoured the glass of twelve-year-old Johnnie Walker whisky as he listened to the old man's vague tales about the neighbourhood and the days when the horse and cart ruled the roads.

In the course of these nostalgic ramblings, Cyril Caddy lit a briar pipe and told his guest that he was a retired dealer in stamps. He pointed with the stem of the btiar towards the array of stamps from every country in the world, framed over the fireplace. His tongue was now well and truly loosened and he talked enthusiastically about Penny Reds and Blacks - the most expensive stamps in the world - as well as the Treskilling Yellow, Inverted Jenny, the Upside-down Swan and other legends of philately.

Caddy eventually became drowsy and John had to tell him to be careful not to drop his pipe on the carpet and set fire to the cottage. Caddy thanked him for the warning and extinguished his pipe. He then apologised for almost dropping off in front of his guest, at which John stood up, thanked him for the excellent hospitality he had shown, shook his hand, stroked Billy's head, and then left to resume his homeward journey.

He had traipsed as far as Broadgreen Road through the now thinning fog, when he suddenly realised that he had left his woollen hat on the armchair in the old man's cottage. The hat had belonged to John's late uncle and was of great sentimental value to him, but it was too cold and too far to go back and get it. So he trudged wearily on until he reached his home on Townsend Lane, where he arrived chilled to the bone.

A few days later, as John was leaving McAlister's Newsagents on Townsend Lane with a copy of the Daily Mirror tucked under his arm and a packet of cigarettes in his pocket, Tommy Birtles, an old friend of his that he had not seen since his schooldays, shouted to him from a shiny and very new-looking Ford Cortina Mk I. "Tommy!" A surprised John shouted back to his old friend. "Look at you in your posh motor!" He then asked him how he could afford a car like that and Tommy just winked and replied with a smirk, "Where there's a will there's a way -"

John had heard rumours about his old friend that he had turned his hand to the occasional burglary since leaving school. Nevertheless, he happily jumped into Tommy's car and they drove around more or less aimlessly for a while as he was shown the finer points of the Cortina. At one point in this rather pointless jaunt, the Cortina was travelling along Thomas Lane in Knotty Ash, when the familiar road jogged John's memory of that foggy night just a few days ago. He recalled that Cyril Caddy's cottage was around there somewhere and perhaps if he could locate it he could call on Mr Caddy and see if he still had the woollen hat.

John finally located the cottage after twenty minutes

of searching, but oddly it was now empty and all its windows boarded-up. He thought he must have come to the wrong address at first, but then he noticed the weathered plaque on the gate - and upon it the faded name 'Cranleigh' in dull traceries of gold. That left him in no doubt that it was Cyril Caddy's cottage.

John told Tommy Birtles all about his adventure that night and how the cottage now seemed empty and abandoned and his friend became intrigued. He approached an elderly woman who was passing and asked her how long the cottage had been boarded up. She stopped and looked at Tommy over the top of her glasses as she leaned on the handle of her walking stick. She looked at the tumbledown cottage in question, then replied, "Ooh, I'm not quite sure, dear - for about twenty years, I think. Yes, a good twenty years." Then she shot alternate glances at Tommy and John, and asked the latter, "Why? Are you thinking of buying it? It must be in a terrible state after being empty for so long." John then stepped forward and told the old woman about Mr Caddy's hospitality of just a few days ago and the pensioner returned a puzzled look. "Like I said, no one's lived there for about twenty years, so it couldn't have been here you were talking about." Then she added, "Old Cyril used to live there, but I think he died around nineteen forty-seven, or maybe forty-eight."

"That was his name!" John cried, his eyes widening with excitement. "He told me his name was Cyril Caddy."

"I never knew what Cyril's second name was, though I used to say hello to him for years. It's a strange one this, isn't it? A bit of a mystery."

The old woman paused for a while, shaking her head, then carried on her way, no doubt turning John's weird account over in her mind as she did so.

John went to the cottage door, lifted the creaky flap of the letterbox and looked inside. He saw something which made him shudder. Down the hallway, on the right-hand side, there was a doorway, and through this doorway he could see into the cottage's living room. There were pages of old yellowed broadsheet newspapers lying here and there on the floorboards, and there, plainly visible on the bare floor, was a blue woollen hat - unmistakably the same hat that John had left at Caddy's cottage just a few days ago.

John's face crumpled as he told Tommy that the hat was of great sentimental importance to him, and seeing this, his friend, who, as we know, had criminal tendencies, returned to the cottage after dark, picked the lock, and retrieved the hat in question. So far so simple, yet for Tommy this break-in was like no other and he afterwards revealed that he had heard strange noises whilst inside that cottage, and had smelt the strong yet fresh aroma of the very same pipe tobacco his father smoked in the living room. In the hallway he had nearly jumped out of his skin when he heard a dog growling, although he could not see it.

John Hollingworth gradually came to accept that the ghost of a man who had been dead for almost twenty years had given him a lift on that freezing foggy night in 1967. What he did not know was that it had all happened before, in 1960, and again in 1962 - both during autumn time.

At 10pm on the Wednesday night of 9 November 1960, twenty-seven-year-old Maureen Wright was standing at a bus stop in Speke, when she received the offer of a lift from an old man who reminded her of her grandfather, driving a large antiquated-looking car. He dropped her off on Pilch Lane close to her home. Throughout the journey the elderly driver did not utter a single word and instead hummed a tune to himself. As Maureen turned to wave to the elderly Samaritan, she watched the car vanish into thin air. A young engaged couple, Alfie Pearson and June Walker, happened to be strolling along Pilch Lane that night, and they too saw the old-fashioned car and its white-haired driver vanish before their eyes.

The other incident took place one Sunday night, in November 1962, when fifty-year old Mrs McGarry left her sister's house off Huyton Lane at 10.30pm, intending to walk home. Mrs McGarry lived on Page Moss Lane, just over a mile from her sister's house, and it took her, on average, about fifteen minutes to reach home. On this particular night, there was a heavy downpour, and by the time she had reached the beginning of Rupert Road, she was practically soaked to the skin. Being a Sunday night, there were hardly any pedestrians about, and the road too was rather quiet, except for the sound of the rain bouncing off the tarmac.

Suddenly, a car came up Rupert Road and stopped just ahead of Mrs McGarry. An old man with white hair leaned over and opened the passenger door and asked her if she needed a lift. Although she was soaked through, and, now a sharp cold wind was blowing in her face, Mrs McGarry said, "No thanks, love. I'll be fine." She had heard too many tales of women coming to grief after accepting lifts from strangers. But the old man persisted, and Mrs McGarry eventually caved in, thinking to herself what harm could such an elderly man possibly do to her. After all, she could have knocked him down with a feather.

Throughout the journey the old man said nothing, which made Mrs McGarry feel a bit edgy, and she was very relieved when the car eventually stopped at the corner of Western Avenue and Page Moss Lane. She could see her home through the vehicle's rain-lashed windscreen, and her husband Jim's silhouette as he waited for her in the living room. The woman thanked the old man then hurried through the downpour to Jim, who said, "Who was that?" as he watched the old fashioned car drive off into the rainy night. Seconds later he did a double take, because one moment it was there, heading towards Pilch Lane, and the next it was nowhere to be seen. However, even in that short space of time, he was able to ascertain that the car was a 1940s Rover - the very same car John Hollingworth would later travel in, on that foggy autumn night in 1967.

Why Cyril Caddy returns to life and offers people lifts in his old Rover car will probably remain one of Liverpool's unsolved mysteries. Caddy represents the classic anniversary ghost, always favouring the autumn months to become active again. Is he even aware that he is dead? Or is he some sort of after-image, or hologram, from the past that lacks consciousness - only as 'real' as an image of some long dead film star on a present day television screen?

SHINING EYES

A fortnight into January, 1965, and fierce gales spiralled around Britain, whipping up the seas around the coasts, causing havoc with shipping and loss of life amongst the fishermen. In the east, Yarmouth ferry services were abandoned; in the south, 86mph gusts were battering the vessels caught in the Channel and bringing floods to Devon. In the north, the gales brought blizzards to Scotland, blocking the three main roads to Glasgow. In the west, the high-speed winds hammered Wales, and the north-west.

Being a port city, Liverpool bore the brunt of these gales and sustained much structural damage. As night fell the vortex tightened and came inland. On Bodmin Road, in Walton, Martha Jones and her twelve-year-old daughter Marie sat in front of the glowing coal fire, appreciating its dancing flames and glowing orange core on such an Arctic night. As the wind whistled down the chimney and rattled the letterbox, mother and daughter were engrossed in an episode of the popular American television series *Dr Kildare*, starring heart-throb actor Richard Chamberlain.

'Marie, you're too close to the fire, girl,' Martha warned. 'You'll have corned-beef legs if you're not careful.'

'What type of legs?' Marie asked with a grin, but lifted the old upright chair she was sitting on and moved it back a few inches from the hearth.

'Chilblains -' her mum explained, '- they make your legs go all mottled like corned-beef.'

Around 8.30pm, Marie thought she heard a voice in the hallway, and went to look. She saw the letterbox open slightly, and it seemed that someone was shining a torch through it.

'Marie, will you shut that door? You're letting all the heat out of the room.'

Marie ran back into the living room trembling. 'There's something outside,' she managed to say.

'There's what outside?' Martha rose from her comfy armchair and turned towards the frightened girl.

'A ghost -' Marie told her mother, and gulped '- and it had glowing eyes.'

Martha got up to see for herself, but Marie screamed for her to stay with her. Martha carried on anyway, switching the light on in the hall and heading towards the door - but she stopped in her tracks. The letterbox flap was now fully open and a pair of glowing, evil-looking eyes was glaring at her through it. Martha nearly jumped out of her skin and cried out, 'Mary, mother of God!'

The eyes had an insane, menacing look about them and Martha backed away — straight into her petrified daughter, and they both let out a yelp. They rushed back into the living room, and Martha closed the door behind her and leaned with her back against it, frightened and confused. She then went over to the fire and gave Marie a hug. They stood there, gazing at the living room door, horrified at the possibility of the entity entering the house and coming through that door. After a few minutes, they heard the front door thud - as if someone had just come in. Footsteps approached, and Marie clung on to her mother. Then the door flew open - but it was only Martha's husband Arthur, back early from the pub, with a parcel of fish and chips in his hands. He laughed when he heard what had frightened them and just unfolded the newspaper and set about his fish and chips, saying in a rather condescending manner, 'Ah, there's no such things as ghosts; you've seen a reflection or something - a trick of the light.'

That night, at around 1.40am, Marie was in bed, sound asleep, when something woke her and she immediately thought of those evil shining eyes peering through the letterbox. She looked at the window. The bedroom curtains had not been drawn, which was unusual, as she usually closed them before getting undressed. That night she had been so weary that she had simply undressed and got straight into bed without closing the curtains.

Marie looked out at the wintry world beyond the windows. Sleet was falling now, and the gale was still wailing like the lament of banshees. She wondered again what those unearthly eyes were, and then tried to drive such thoughts from her mind. Instead, she concentrated on the stories she had read earlier in *The Bunty*, a comic aimed at girls of her age. As Marie sleepily dwelt on the characters her nervousness evaporated and she closed her eyes.

As she did so a body fell on the bed!

Marie's eyelids flew open - just in time to see the

silhouette of a man's body bounce off her mattress and roll across the room after hitting the floor with a ghastly-sounding thud. Marie felt unreal, as if she were dreaming, and her whole body from head to toe was numb as she got out of the bed and ran to her mother and father's room. They were already sitting up in bed when Marie reached them, because they'd too had been woken by the loud thump of the body hitting the bedroom floor next door.

'What the bleedin' hell is going on?' Marie's father demanded.

She switched on the light and told him about the man who had fallen on to her bed. He had hit the bed so hard, his head had smashed into Marie's lower leg as he landed on her. She rubbed her calf- it hurt.

Mother and father investigated and found no one in Marie's bedroom. 'You probably fell out of bed after having a nightmare,' opined Marie's Dad, but she knew what she had seen, and felt, and she had definitely not been dreaming. The schoolgirl slept very uneasily for the remainder of that wintry night with her bedside lamp on.

Five nights later, Martha and Marie were once again watching television, and the time was approaching 9pm, and already Arthur was gazing in the mirror, adjusting his tie as he got ready to pop out to his local - The Winslow Hotel, on Goodison Road. He was in the middle of slicking back his Brylcreemed hair when a familiar thud was heard upstairs - again in Marie's room.

'What was that?' cried Martha in alarm, jumping out of her comfy armchair and rushing over to the television to turn down the *Danny Kaye Show*. 'Stay there!' said Arthur and went to investigate. He searched every room, starting with Marie's, but found nothing amiss. When he came back downstairs, he said it had probably been someone in the street shutting a car door. Martha and Marie did not buy that explanation, and Arthur left his wife and daughter in the house to go to the pub, knowing full well that they were both feeling on edge, but he was selfish that way.

Later that evening, just before 11pm, the glowing eyes appeared again as Marie was in the hallway, off to bed. She saw the tell-tale glow through the semi-circular frosted window of the front door, followed by the lifting of the letterbox. On this occasion, a woman who lived opposite also saw the glowing eyes, visible as two bright points. The lights hovered in front of Martha's door, then suddenly flitted sideways and across the road, before vanishing down an alleyway at the end of Bodmin Road, which faced the gates of Anfield Cemetery.

Weeks later, Marie's best friend Laura home one Saturday evening - February 13 to be precise - the eve of Valentine's Day. Marie told her about the shining eyes and the phantom body that had fallen on top of her, and Laura, excited by these accounts, foolishly suggested holding a séance to contact any spirits; 'Perhaps they could tell us who we'll marry,' she suggested. Marie was not keen on the idea, but Laura eventually talked her into it.

The two girls watched one of their favourite television programmes first - *Jukebox Jury* - in which a panel of celebrities judged new pop-songs. The show began at a quarter-past five, and ended at twenty-to-six, when Martha made the tea for her husband, daughter and Laura. By 6pm, darkness had fallen, and after the tea, the girls retreated to Marie's bedroom to dabble in the supernatural, equipped with a candle and a box of matches. The candle was lit and the light switched off. Outside, a waxing gibbous moon was casting its pale silvery-grey light into the bedroom, so the curtains were drawn tight to block it out. The girls sat at a green baize card table belonging to Arthur. Candle wax was accidentally spilt on the baize, and Marie knew her father would have something to say about that. Laura sat facing her and the distorted shadows of the two schoolgirls danced about on the walls and ceiling as the candle flame flickered. Laura rapped on the green baize in time to a popular football chant that featured LFC player Ian St John: 'One-two, one-two-three, one-two-three-four - Saint John!'

'Knock twice if there's anybody there,' whispered Marie, putting a brave face on the spooky proceedings, and she gave a hollow little forced laugh.

Laura tapped out that football rhyme again: 'One-two, one-two-three, one-two-three-four -'

Two very loud knocks drowned out the words 'Saint John' and shook the walls of the room. Moments later, as the girls sat looking at one another in silent shock, Marie's mother thumped the handle of her mop against the ceiling downstairs in protest at the loud thumps she had heard up in her daughter's room. All of a sudden, Laura's eyes widened and a look of pure terror formed on her face, as she stared directly at Marie.

'Laura what's wrong?' Marie asked.

Laura screamed and the candle went out.

Both girls made a beeline for the door, Marie

knocking over the card table as she went. Shrieking female laughter echoed about the darkness as if the room were an enormous cavern. The door was yanked open and Laura fell over Marie and landed with a thump on the landing. Marie's mother shouted up the stairs: 'Eh! Pack it in up there!'

Laura ran out of the house without stopping for any goodbyes, or explanations as to what had freaked her out up in the room. However, on the following day when Marie visited her at her home on Stanley Park Avenue, Laura told her exactly what she had seen. During their botched séance, Laura had seen Marie's face gradually change, until it had become snow white, and her eyes heavily bordered in black and taken on a tear-drop shape. Even her eyebrows and hair had altered, both becoming jet black, until she looked like a Geisha girl. That metamorphosis - known in the world of the paranormal as 'transfiguration' - had terrified the life out of Laura, though Marie's face had returned to normal as soon as she left the bedroom.

A few years after these strange happenings, Marie and her parents left the house on Bodmin Road, but the new tenants got an unwelcome surprise when they moved into what appears to be a haunted residence. The grandfather of the new family sadly died just a fortnight after moving to Bodmin Road, and being Irish and of the Catholic faith, they decided to hold a wake. The grandfather was laid out in a splendid open coffin in the front parlour, where friends and families were free to come and pay their last respects.

Two former neighbours of the deceased - a Mr Loughlin and a Mrs Sullivan - turned up at the house on the eve of the funeral to pray close to the body of their old friend. The time was 9.30pm and as the two mourners silently prayed, they heard a faint voice in the parlour, and it seemed to be coming from the deceased. Mr Loughlin tilted his head and put his ear close to the corpse's head. He was shocked and a little perturbed to hear a faint female voice reciting an old nursery rhyme. Loughlin beckoned Mrs Sullivan to come closer to the coffin, and she also heard the eerie whispering voice, singing:

Hickory dickory dock,
The mouse ran up the clock -

Both of the mourners trembled as they realised that the voice was emanating from the closed mouth of the dead man. Loughlin and Sullivan shrank back from the coffin and left the house in a distressed state. They went at once to the presbytery to fetch a Catholic priest. When the priest visited the house on Bodmin Road he was to hear several accounts of alleged supernatural occurrences that had taken place there from different members of the family. One of these accounts told of a pair of glowing eyes that were seen looking through an upstairs window. The priest went around the house, blessing each room in turn, and no more whispers were heard from the corpse. The funeral went ahead the following morning without incident.

I have researched the history of the house on Bodmin Road and cannot find any event or piece of information regarding its former occupiers which would throw some light on the shining eyes, the falling body, or the nursery rhyme whispers from a dead man's lips. Perhaps one day, if strange happenings once again unfold at the address, we may be able to discover just what is behind the haunted house of Walton's Bodmin Road.

Printed in Great Britain
by Amazon